Astute new voices with fresh vision carrying the torch forward for the Sacred Feminine. Excited by the rich diversity between two covers. Touches many of the bases.
Karen Tate, author, *Goddess Calling* and *Voices of the Sacred Feminine*

An exciting look at the many faces of Goddess in America, from the indigenous and the imported, to the "rewritten" goddesses. Also covered: Goddess as perceived variously by American feminists, psychologists, shamans, Christians, and others. Highly informative and well written.
Jerri Studebaker, author, *Switching to Goddess* and *Breaking the Mother Goose Code*

In this book you'll find some of the most articulate and forward-thinking voices in the current generation of American Pagan writers. Writers in this volume like Daimler, Telyndru, and Moss, deserve to be as 'household' in the Pagan world as predecessors like Starhawk and Ravenwolf. With their serious yet loving look at where American Paganism came from and where it should be going, I have no doubt the contributors in this book will fruitfully influence the Paganism of the world.
Brendan Myers, author, *The Earth, The Gods and The Soul - A History of Pagan Philosophy*

The Goddess religion in contemporary America is a growing and very necessary spiritual movement in a country where there has never yet (as I write this) been a female head of state. Forty percent of American households are run by women who are the sole provider, yet women still make seventy nine cents for every dollar an American man makes. American women find themselves in a warrior society with a strong culture of guns and exploitation of the Earth, and are barely beginning to reclaim the status their ancestral mothers once enjoyed when Goddesses shared the dais with Gods.

Within these pages we learn of Native American Goddesses who teach the lessons of humility, self-sacrifice and connection to the Earth and her creatures. Also the awareness that the sacred feminine dwells within the soil and the Moon, meaning that abuse of the Earth is essentially the same thing as abuse of the Goddess.

We read about the spiritual plight of the immigrant; America has always been an immigrant society and American women who seek a Goddess must decide whether to adopt the native Goddesses of this land, invent a completely new path, or honor their own ancient lineage based on their distant DNA.

We hear from the Reconstructionists who urge us to speak to a Goddess in her own language, whatever it may be, because words have power and this is a way to honor a deity. We are cautioned to read primary sources, give back to the culture we are learning from, and make the effort to visit sacred sites connected to a particular Goddess, no matter how far away they might be.

We taste a bit of Voodoo, Minoan religion, Hebrew and Canaanite Goddess tradition. The Christian Divine Mother finds her place in these pages, as does Brighid; the Mary of the Gael.

We read of modern media Goddesses like Marilyn Monroe and Angelina Jolie, and see powerful Goddess archetypes within strong women such as Amelia Earhart, Harriet Tubman and Eleanor Roosevelt.

No sex-drunk nymphs enter these pages. The Goddess of the Witches and Druids emerges as a powerful eco-feminist. Her Priestesses are mature champions of social justice; healers and ritualists and weavers of radical change for their community.

This is a necessary book for the times we live in.

Ellen Evert Hopman, is Archdruid of Tribe of the Oak www.tribe-oftheoak.com and the author of *A Legacy of Druids – Conversations with Druid Leaders of Britain, the USA and Canada, Secret Medicines from Your Garden – Plants for Healing, Spirituality & Magic* and other volumes. Find her books and blog at www.elleneverthopman.com

The Goddess
in America
The Divine Feminine in Cultural Context

The Goddess in America

The Divine Feminine in Cultural Context

Edited by Trevor Greenfield

Winchester, UK
Washington, USA

First published by Moon Books, 2016
Moon Books is an imprint of John Hunt Publishing Ltd., Laurel House, Station Approach,
Alresford, Hants, SO24 9JH, UK
office1@jhpbooks.net
www.johnhuntpublishing.com
www.moon-books.net

For distributor details and how to order please visit the 'Ordering' section on our website.

Text copyright: Trevor Greenfield 2015

ISBN: 978 1 78279 925 2
978-1-78279-924-5 (e-book)
Library of Congress Control Number: 2016943147

A CIP catalogue record for this book is available from the British Library.

Design: Stuart Davies
Original Cover design by Freya Greenfield

Printed and bound by CPI Group (UK) Ltd, Croydon, CR0 4YY, UK

We operate a distinctive and ethical publishing philosophy in all
areas of our business, from our global network of authors to
production and worldwide distribution.

CONTENTS

Introduction

A melting pot of nations. A cauldron of cultures. A medicine bundle of traditions and peoples brought together from around the world.

Those of us who dwell in North America are both blessed and burdened by the spiritual legacies of the indigenous peoples of the land where we dwell, the spiritual traditions of the lands from which our ancestors may have emigrated, and the call to create new iterations of spirituality in the collective matrix of the here and the now of modern American culture. These can be confusing waters to navigate, and the collection of essays in this volume speaks to the various currents of exploration and concern that define present-day Goddess worship and Neo-Pagan practice in a place where a confluence of many streams of wisdom collect in a way that both seeks to remain connected to original threads of tradition while also, by necessity, weaving an entirely new tapestry of experience.

The United States of America has been called 'The Great Experiment' and was born out of a desire of the nation's founders to forge a new paradigm which, unlike the Europe of their time, did away with old class structures, allowed for freedom of religious expression, and placed more power in the hands of the people by embracing a democratic model of governance. A nation of emigrants, the coming together of peoples from many lands seeking a chance at a better life is part of what has made America strong. Unfortunately, this vision came at a great cost for the indigenous peoples of this continent who were displaced and demonized, and whose rich cultures and very way of life were destroyed as mostly European settlers made their way west. In Canada, attempts at assimilating First Nations people lead to the loss of much of their culture, and often, their children, to this tragically violent colonial mindset. Similarly, in Mexico, Central,

Jhenah Telyndru holds a master's degree in Celtic Studies from the University of Wales, Trinity Saint David. She is the founder of the Sisterhood of Avalon, and her published works include *Avalon Within: A Sacred Journey of Myth, Mystery, and Inner Wisdom* and *The Avalonian Oracle: Wisdom from the Holy Isle*. Jhenah welcomes your contact through her website: www.ynysafallon.com.

Part 1

The Native Goddess

The Influence of Matriarchal American Indian Tribes on the Goddess Movement

After our planet had been divided between water and ground, when the universe had begun to vibrate with the sound of the Creator, in the time when the First World was being born, Spider Woman made the plants, trees, flowers, birds and animals that would call Earth their home. She molded them from clay, wove each of them a white cape, and then sang their Creation Song to make them living. After this, Spider Woman made the first humans, in four pairs, from yellow, red, white, and black earth. She sang the first peoples their Creation Song, and their white cape was the mantle of creative wisdom. She introduced them to the Creator in the red light of dawn and told them always to remember the time of their creation.
— Hopi creation story

The story of Goddess in America is a story of beginnings, of a world being reborn as feminine power is reawakened. The Goddess speaks everywhere to everyone, and she is certainly not new, but it was in North America in the latter twentieth century that industrialized, Christianized people began hearing her voice in significant numbers. Some early sparks of inspiration came from the British Isles, through the work of people such as Dion Fortune and Doreen Valiente, yet this is where the Goddess Movement caught fire. To understand why it happened here and not elsewhere we need to look at the cultural influence of America's indigenous peoples.

The 'Goddess Movement' is a loosely knit international group of women, and a few men, who are making a female deity (or deities) the central part of their spiritual practice and belief. It is not a religion or group of religions per se. While various offshoots of Wicca are often assumed to be part of the Goddess Movement, groups that compulsorily invoke a God for every

6

Goddess to achieve their perception of balance would not be considered 'Goddessian,' or part of the Goddess Movement. Similarly, while Christianity as a whole is antithetical to the beliefs and values of the Goddess Movement, individuals who center the Virgin Mary or Sophia in their spiritual practice may be considered Goddessian. Being part of the Goddess Movement does require, however, that the participant is feminist in their political/spiritual orientation. For most Goddessians, this means endorsing the concept of matriarchy.

As the term is used in the Goddess Movement, 'matriarchy' is not a feminine version of patriarchy, with women dominating and oppressing men: it is a complete antithesis of patriarchy, without exploitation on the basis of sex. Matriarchal societies are peaceful, devoid of class structure, and egalitarian in their distribution of wealth. They emphasize the importance of a mother deity, rather than enforcing the illogic of a father-god birthing the universe.

'Matriarchy' is perhaps an unfortunate word choice, because it tends to be applied in a general sense to situations where women have more power than men are comfortable with. Archaeologists in the nineteenth century, encountering a plethora of female votive images in their excavations of Neolithic Europe, concluded that the societies these images came from were not patriarchal and therefore labeled them 'matriarchal.' Today we understand that women in these late Stone Age societies were probably not dominating men, despite the preponderance of feminine iconography, and the Goddessian interpretation of 'matriarchy' has evolved. Other words have been proposed, such as gynarchy, gylany, gynandry, or gynocracy, but they have not caught on. I think the affinity Goddessians have for the word matriarchy stems from the root matri-, which means 'mother.' Appreciation for the creating/generating power of the feminine divine is integral to the Goddess Movement.

At the start of the colonial era none of the nations of the

7

Americas perfectly conformed to the idealized Goddessian concept of matriarchy, yet all were considerably less patriarchal than the European cultures they came in contact with. Among the more matriarchal North American societies that early explorers and settlers encountered were the Taino of the Caribbean, the first tribe of the Western Hemisphere to receive the appellation 'Indian,' who entrusted considerable political power to women and were noted for their generosity; the Huichol of west central Mexico, who had a cosmology with a preponderance of feminine deities and who resisted Catholic syncretism; the Delaware communities of the mid-Atlantic region, who had an egalitarian social structure and a flexible understanding of gender; and the Iroquois Six Nations, who had a well-developed system of government with powerful women's councils. These are but a few of many examples.

Many are unaware of the impact of aboriginal peoples on American values and culture, and most believe Native participation in American history has been limited to waging war and relinquishing territory. It is true that European conquest imposed a patriarchal mindset on Native spiritual, economic, and political structures, and that it resulted in dispossession of land, population, livelihood, spiritual practices, self-governance, and even language, but it is a fallacy to believe the cultural impact always went one way. Areas of Native influence include loan words from the pidgin Algonquin that was the lingua franca for the first century of European settlement; medicine based on plants indigenous to North America; more liberal child-rearing practices; more positive attitudes toward bathing; and cultivation of unfamiliar foods that today make up a large proportion of the American diet.

Native influence on the establishment of American democracy is especially instructive in understanding later contribution to the Goddess Movement. The Founding Fathers who incited the overthrow of British monarchy and composed the documents that established the American government had a Classical education and were inspired by their idealization of the democracies of Greece and Rome. However, at the start of the American Revolution the Roman Republic had been dead for more than 1,800 years. It would be audacious in the extreme for any sane person to read about a remote democracy in a book and then proceed to organize a rebellion against the king, trusting that the installment of a subsequent autocrat was in no way inevitable. Perhaps Benjamin Franklin, Thomas Jefferson, John Adams and others had that audacity, but they did not need to depend entirely on ancient history for support. British America had grown up alongside Amerindian nations that practiced self-government, in some cases through confederacies that encompassed large numbers of people. The degree to which specific Native governments modeled the American Constitution is contentious, but there can be no doubt that there was some influence. Most importantly, contact with Amerindian nations ensured that Americans fighting to establish a democratic government were not fighting for an ideal that was nebulous and abstract, but one they understood.

There were similarly strong Native contributions to the abolitionist and socialist movements, but Native influence on American feminism is especially pertinent to understanding the Goddess Movement. Colonial interaction with Iroquois and Algonquin tribes puts the words of Abigail Adams to her husband at the eve of the American Revolution in a more understandable context. 'If perticuliar care and attention is not paid to the Laidies,' she wrote, 'we are determined to foment a Rebelion, and will not hold ourselves bound by any Laws in which we have no voice, or Representation.' The 'Laidies' knew that women did have representation in the aboriginal governments, which the Founding Fathers looked to for validation, but they suspected this was about to be written out of the next government. (John Adams wrote his wife back saying in effect that she was cute when she was angry.)

American women continued to foment, albeit below the surface, into the nineteenth century, and if the Seneca Falls convention in 1848 is taken as the official start of the American feminist movement, there was a long prodromal period. A taste of what was coming was presaged by the publication almost fifteen years earlier of Lydia Maria Child's *History of the Condition of Women, in Various Ages and Nations*, which elucidated the differences between Iroquois cultures and European patriarchies. The abolitionist movement in general, and the writings of Mary Wollstonecraft and Michel de Montaigne in particular, are rightly credited as an inspiration for American feminism, but critical collaboration with Native women is often overlooked. Feminism received support not only through formal associations, theoretical writings, and individual heroics, but also through living examples. Native Americans lived what American feminists preached.

Many participants in what is now called the First Wave of feminism understood Christianity to be a major stumbling block for women's emancipation. The culmination of half a century of scholarship on Christian patriarchy was the 1898 publication of *The Woman's Bible*, in which Elizabeth Cady Stanton, the head of the Revising Committee, as it called itself, declared: 'The Bible in its teachings degrades Woman from Genesis to Revelations.' Matilda Joslyn Gage, responding to accusations of sacrilege on the part of the Committee, averred that 'our present quest is not what the mystic or the spiritual character of the Bible may be; we are investigating its influence on woman under Judaism and Christianity, and pronounce it evil.'

Gage went beyond biblical criticism to explore positive religious and social roles for women in non-Christian societies. She looked at pre-Christian Western societies and found what she termed 'the Matriarchate or Mother-rule.' In the matriarchate, woman embodied the foundations of religion: 'The primal priest on earth, she was also supreme as Goddess in heaven.' Gage further asserted that the matriarchate had survived into modern times:

Every part of the world today gives evidence of the system; reminiscences of the Matriarchate everywhere abound. Livingstone found African tribes swearing by the mother and tracing descent through her. Marco Polo discovered similar customs in his Asiatic voyages, and the same customs are extant among the Indians of our own continent.

That the same customs were extant in America Gage knew through direct contact. An advocate for Native as well as women's rights, she cultivated friendships was Iroquois women, as did other feminist spokeswomen. Gage was eventually adopted into the tribe's Wolf Clan and Council of Matrons.

Though Gage was considered a radical embarrassment by many in the suffrage movement, feminists of the twentieth century Second Wave were also cognizant of Christianity's link with women's subordination and were quick to dust off her work. By this time fresh scholarship was available, such as Robert Graves' analysis of how the Greek myths had been perverted under patriarchy and Marija Gimbutas' archaeological investigation of Neolithic 'Old Europe.' A huge backlash in academia ensued, which continues unabated to this day, dedicated to burying the notion of matriarchy. The term became defined in the most stringent of ways, with all historical and archaeological evidence supporting the existence of non-patriarchal societies being dismissed as 'speculative' – this by scholars who had no problem positing theories on warfare with far more tenuous data. The vast work by Graves was submitted to a microscope, with each small error gleefully trumpeted, while his writing as a whole was derided as specious on the basis that his critics disagreed with it.

But even before this backlash had time to mobilize, spiritual feminists needed something more. It was one thing to read about matriarchy in a book; it was another to seriously propose it. Living forms of Goddess worship existed, such as the cults of the Virgin Mary or the Hindu and Buddhist Goddesses, but such deities were worshiped in a theological context that subordinated the divine feminine to the divine masculine, and the condition of women in societies that venerated these Goddesses contrasted sharply with these images. Matriarchal roots to these religions could and would be explored, but the immediate need was for models of worship in societies where women had power. Native American traditional societies were not the only models American feminists could have found, but these were the ones that were most accessible.

Discussing the contribution of a Native perspective to the Goddess Movement is perhaps objectionable to some, given that it is debatable whether cultures indigenous to this hemisphere, outside of Mesoamerica, even operate within a 'Goddess' framework. Part of the confusion lies with the stark demarcation in Western culture between mundane and divine, a distinction absent in most indigenous cosmologies. Words for woman in aboriginal languages may carry significantly different connotations than in the Indo-European languages. Native spiritual beings are usually translated into English with words such as woman, maiden, grandmother, or boy, when a gender is denoted at all. (Sex-specific markers may not be highly prevalent in the language or story, yet characters are often rendered as male in English.) Still, the divine persons in Native mythologies have analogous roles to Goddessian deities, even if the translations are challenging.

Feminists were drawn with most alacrity to indigenous concepts of female spiritual societies operating in tandem with co-ed and men's societies; menarche ceremonies and spiritual cosmologies dignifying menstruation; the mother clan rather than marriage operating as the basic family unit; respect for female authority rather than isolation and denigration of old women; and women as visionaries, dreamers and interpreters of myth. Native women elders spoke at Goddess gatherings, memoirs by Native women were enthusiastically received, tattered copies of collected Amerindian stories were passed along, and contemporary artwork depicting heroines from Native legends became popular.

It is important to understand Native American influence on the Goddess Movement on a comprehensive level rather than trying to trace specific ceremonies, symbols, healing practices, and myths. In many cases a ceremony or practice was never integrated into other frameworks because it was too culturally specific or unsuitable for an industrial society, but the ideas it carried nevertheless inspired reflection. Some legends had general appeal while others did not, yet there was still something to learn from them. The transmission of ideas, so taken for granted in the world of men, is often denied as a reality among women. Our world supposedly exists on the level of upholding traditions and trading recipes: we carry the family stories; we do not add to a body of knowledge or enable it to grow.

The Goddess Movement is no longer an American, or even a Western, phenomenon. It has spread around the world and has gained a foothold in places including India, Nigeria and South Korea. Matriarchal cultures are being studied in other parts of the world, such as western China, bringing new lived experiences to the concept of a matriarchy nourished by a loving Mother-Goddess. I wonder if the role of indigenous Americans in helping to birth this reawakening will be remembered, or if the Native role in this origin story is destined to become obscured like so many others.

A standard line in academia, perilous to cross, says 'there is no evidence' that matriarchies ever existed. Each aboriginal American culture can be scrutinized and found wanting in some respect, or when that fails dismissed as being too fragmentary to be conclusive. Yet the same cynical principle that is applied to matriarchy could also be applied to democracy. Extinct Stone Age civilizations could be ignored for not providing definitive data, the flaws in the so-called democracies of Athens and Rome could be magnified, the aboriginal self-government strategies of the Americas could be categorized as below criteria, and modern approximations of democracy could be dismissed as unstable and non-egalitarian. But we don't dismiss democracy as a whimsical chimera indulged in by flighty and unserious people. We treat it as something real, imperfect as it is, and take actions to improve participation in practice as well as theory. Goddessians see through the self-serving cynicism of the patriarchy and are not swayed from their matriarchal vision.

We are all children of the Great Mother, men as well as women, whether we call her First Woman, Goddess, Queen of Heaven, or Eve. All journeys lead from her and she is at the end of every road. To dishonor her is to reject a part of ourselves, and so a world where feminine leadership is ubiquitous is not only good and right and sensible; it is inevitable. We know our history and so we can see our future. With gratitude we acknowledge the first peoples of Turtle Island, and all peoples of the world, who hold this truth. *Aho.*

Hearth Moon Rising was born in Ohio and is of Irish, German-Appalachian, and Delaware Indian descent. She is the author of *Invoking Animal Magic: A Guide for the Pagan Priestess*. She lives in the Adirondacks of northern New York and blogs at hearthmoonblog.com.

Cherokee

The Old Stories

The Cherokee, or Tsalagi, which refers to the language of the tribe Tsalagi Gawonihisdi, were originally called the Aniyunwiya. The Aniyunwiya believed that they had once belonged to a distant land, one far from North America, and that they traveled here because their people grew in population so as to be unable to remain in the old land. In their journey, the land went from snow-covered mountains to the place where the sun sets. (This version of the migration myth was published in *A Cherokee Migration Fragment* by Corkran, circa 1717.) This story seems to be in agreement with the theories of some scholars who believe that any human inhabitants migrated to the Americas after the ice age via a land bridge that once extended from Asia.

Creation

Perhaps more importantly, prior to the migration story, there was creation. The Tsalagi creation stories do not usually begin with human beings. Rather, it was the animals who brought forth the earth. Given the great respect of and toward animals as siblings rather than lesser creatures, this version reflects a perspective of the interconnectedness of the world and all of its things.

Plants and animals were the first created, humans came later. In the beginning, there was only a brother and a sister (First Man and First Woman), but the brother struck the sister with a fish and told her to multiply. In seven days, she bore a child. And, every seven days thereafter, a new child was born to her. Their population grew so quickly that they were afraid the earth couldn't hold them, so a woman became able to have only one child a year.

James Mooney gathered this version, which was published by the Bureau of American Ethnology (1900):

When all was water the animals were above in Galun lati, beyond the arch; but it was very much crowded, and they were wanting more room. They wondered what was below the water, and at last Dayuni si, 'Beaver's Grandchild,' the little water-beetle, offered to go and see if it could learn. It darted in every direction over the surface of the water, but could find no firm place to rest. Then it dived to the bottom and came up with some soft mud, which began to grow and spread on every side until it became the island which we call earth. It was afterward fastened to the sky with four cords, but no one remembers who did this.

At first, the earth was flat and very soft and wet. The animals were anxious to get down, and sent out different birds to see if it was yet dry, but they found no place to alight and came back again to Galun lati. At last, it seemed to be time and they sent out Buzzard and told him to go and make ready for them. This was the Great Buzzard, the father of all buzzards we see now.

He flew all over the earth, low down near the ground, and it was still soft. When he reached the Cherokee country, he was very tired, and his wings began to flap and strike the ground, and wherever they struck the earth there was a valley, and where they turned up again there was a mountain. When the animals above saw this, they were afraid the whole world would be mountains, so they called him back, but the Cherokee country remains full of mountains today.

There is the belief, as well, that another world lives under the first, which is exactly the same, save the seasons, which are reversed. So, there were three worlds – the one above the sky arch (the arc that the sun travels daily in the sky), the middle world where humans lived, and the lower world, which was opposite the middle world. The above and below worlds contain powerful spirit beings who were in direct opposition with each other. It was, therefore, the primary responsibility of the middle world to maintain balance and harmony in all things.

This pattern of balance and harmony is repeated throughout most of the stories of the Cherokee people. The origins of disease are, in fact, another of these lessons in balance: Men created weapons – bows and knives, spears, hooks, and other things – which made it easier for them to kill their feathered and furred cousins. Men overpopulated and became greedy, killing when they had no need for food. They lost respect for the smaller creatures, smashing them beneath their feet without concern. The animals gathered and, angered and hurt by the betrayal, devised diseases to manage the population of man. Were it not for the plant people, who were able to cure some of these diseases, all humans may have died out.

Woman

Being a matrilineal clan, the Cherokee woman has a high level of importance. The clan mothers often made decisions that are currently made by modern-day governments, including police actions. If a woman is of the Wolf clan, she will always be (regardless of marriage or her husband's clan affiliation) and so will her children. The woman owned all property, including any farming plots and homes. Should a woman wish their husband to leave, she had only to put his hunting and ceremonial tools out of the home.

It stands to reason, then, that the most important crop of the people would come from the body of a woman. Corn Mother, called Selu (pronounced Say-loo) by the Tsalagi, exists in many Native cultures. In most, she is the giver of life, the provider of nourishment, the sacrificial lamb of the peoples. There are many versions of the story from many tribes, perhaps the best known of the Corn Mother tales is the Penobscot version where the Corn Mother had to die to provide food for the people. It goes something like this:

Corn Mother was very sad because the people had grown so large. They were multiplying and hungry, unable to have the earth sustain them. Corn Mother wept and could not stop. Her husband was saddened at her state and wanted to make her happy again. He asked Corn Mother what he could do to gladden her. She replied that he must kill her. He refused. She sought the assistance of the Great Mystery, the 'All Maker,' to help her. The All Maker told the husband that he must follow Corn Mother's wishes. When they returned home, he waited until the sun was at its apex in the sky, and did as she asked, caressing her beautiful, silky hair in his hands.

Her two sons were instructed to drag her body back and forth until her flesh was scraped from her bones onto the empty parts of the earth. They left for seven moons. When they returned, they found corn plants with silky tassels like their mother's beautiful hair. The corn was the transformed flesh of Corn Mother. And the people were fed. Because they saved some of the kernels to return to the earth each season, Corn Mother's spirit was renewed, honoring her sacrifice to sustain her children.

The Cherokee version is slightly different:

Selu, the Corn Mother, lived in the forest with her husband, Kanati ('The Lucky Hunter'), and son. Each day, Kanati would go into the woods and return with meat for their family. Each evening, Selu would take the meat to the river where she would clean it and wash the blood into the water. Their son would follow Selu to the river to play along its banks while she worked. After each day's play, the boy would describe another child – a young boy – with whom he would spend his playtime.

In concern, Selu and Kanati followed their son on his play, one day. They found the other boy, who they realized had arisen from the discarded blood of the game that fed their family. They caught the boy and brought him into their home, naming him Inage Utasuhi ('He Who Grew Up Wild'). The boys became inseparable and had many adventures, often finding trouble at the suggestion of Inage Utasuhi.

On one of these occasions, Inage Utasuhi became curious about how and where Kanati found such good game, each day. So, the boys followed Kanati when he left to hunt, one morning, to a cave. As the boys hid, Kanati removed a large rock at the mouth of the cave. A doe emerged and Kanati shot it with an arrow. After replacing the rock to close the cave, Kanati threw the doe over his shoulder, and carried it home to Selu.

Several days later, the boys returned to the cave. They removed the rock as they'd seen their father do. Out came a deer, but they weren't quick enough to shoot it. Disappointed with their lack of skill, they forgot to close the cave. All of the animals escaped and scattered across the lands, making hunting much harder for all people. This left the boys hungry.

In their desire for food, they followed their mother to her vegetable hut, as she went to fetch the corn and beans. When they secreted after her, they saw her rub her stomach and underarms, squatting, creating the corn and beans from her body. They knew, then, that she must be a tsigili (witch) and that they would have to kill her, for they didn't understand the creation that sprung from her flesh.

But, in her knowing way, Selu was aware the boys were plotting her death. She instructed them to kill her, drag her body through the field before burying it, and to keep watch overnight on the ground. The sons, who later became known as the Thunder Boys, did as they were asked. In the morning, maize had begun to grow.

The Lessons

What could be clearer than those lessons demonstrated by Selu, First Woman, and the animal-guided creation and disease origin stories of the Cherokee? The highest need for respect and harmony exist throughout each story. Without the human defects of greed, overpopulation (lust), and ego (killing and stomping upon our fellow creatures), there would be no illness. It was only the pity of the plant people, who better understood the need for balance than their angry and ill-treated animal brethren, which saved humankind from desolation. In other words, left to our own devices, we forget that we are, in fact, connected to all things – no better, no worse, no more or less important. Unlike the perspective of some belief systems, where humans are the stewards of all things, the Tsalagi understood that they were merely another cog in the mechanism.

And, perhaps, most importantly, they knew that they did not (and need not) understand all things. It is common to hear that 'no one remembers' who first completed a task, such as tying the four cardinal points to anchor the earth in its place above the water. Nor is it uncommon in Tsalagi stories to hear reference to the All Maker, or Unetlanvhi ('Creator'), who has no human form, no gender, or personification. The All Maker is merely a knowing force, which guides all things, having made all things.

We, as humans, are not meant to know all. Acceptance of this makes us able to remain in our proper place in the circle of life. Forgetting it brings forth our baser tendencies. We can clearly see the application of human ego and the destruction it brings – war, discrimination, wastefulness – but, most certainly, it brings separation. When we become ego-centered, we become separate. And, when we are separate, we stand alone. Allow that knowledge to settle down. It is a deep knowing.

Selu understands in a sense akin to a sage that her purpose can be accomplished in more than one manner. Knowing that her death is imminent, whether at the hands of her husband or her sons, she recognizes that her function will continue without her physical presence. She is willing to sacrifice for the good of her people, as her ego has not become so large that their lives have lost consequence to her. Selu is willing to be killed in order to provide. What does this say? That we should encourage suicide missions? Hunger strikes? It does not. Instead, it again recognizes the interconnectedness of all things. Selu will no longer be able to provide fruit from her own body, but will ensure the survival of her people for all time. She is a cog in the mechanism.

When we are connected, we co-operate with others. We collaborate and, yes, we sacrifice. We must in order to live within our environment rather than to exploit it, as modern-day humans have been trained to do. The earth is of the same flesh as the mother's body. Both are womb to all things – transforming seed into fruit. Selu can be compared to any other mother figure among the Goddesses of many cultures – Demeter, Frigga, Rhiannon. In each story, there is love, nurturing, transformation, and sacrifice.

And, let us not forget another lesson of the Tsalagi stories – impermanence. Nothing exists eternally in its original form. Selu was transformed into the fields of maize, endlessly renewed through care and replanting. When the earth becomes tired, in the Tsalagi creation myth, the cords will break, the people will die, and the earth will return to the sea. We will not remain, unchanged. Transformation is inevitable. What shall you leave behind?

Today

How can we apply the lessons today?

Should we struggle and fight to maintain the status quo? Does this make sense, knowing whatever we do that all things shall change? Heraclitus is credited with saying, 'The only thing that is constant is change.' And, so it is. Can we learn to embrace our own transformation? Can we release the desire for eternal youth and strength as we wane and return to the womb of our mother earth?

Do we understand where we fit in the mechanism of the circle of life? Do we recognize that we are, in fact, a small part of the whole; and that our own connection to each and every thing we touch (seen and unseen) affects the entire working?

Do we know that, when we become infected by our own self-importance, we are alone, separated from the mechanisms that bind us to each other and all things? How do we find our place in the circle? Do we have the strength to take it? What are we willing to sacrifice?

So, today, there are questions rather than answers. For, as the Tsalagi well know, we cannot know all things, but such insight must be discovered from a place of deep awareness within each of us. We must quest our own truth, as seekers have always done, spending time in quiet contemplation with the support of those we trust.

The Goddesses are within us – hair streaming or short, skin bronzed or fair, limbs willowy or full. If you wish to find Selu in your life, look in the mirror. What things have you birthed? What seeds do you hold? What is your purpose?

Michele L. Warch, MCC, is a 2nd degree priestess in the Sisters of the Spiral Moon coven, an eco-feminist, writer, blogger, mother, wife, and grandmother. A long-time practitioner (including 30-plus years of solitary practice), her specialty areas are as an oneicritic, healer, and facilitator. Michele resides on the Mid-Atlantic coast of the USA with her husband of life-times, where she teaches and writes. Her passion is the recognition, reverence, and return of the Divine Feminine to the world.

Hopi

Soaring more than 8,000 feet at its highest point, and covering four thousand square miles, Black Mesa sprawls through the arid highlands of northeastern Arizona. Jutting from the southern edge of the Black Mesa plateau, three features dominate the landscape. They are known quite simply as First Mesa, Second Mesa, and Third Mesa. It is around and on top of these remote mesas that an ancient and hardy people thrive in the harsh environment, much as they have for thousands of years. Their name is the Hopituh-Shi-nu-mu, 'the peaceful people,' and they are often considered the oldest of the native peoples in North America.

The Hopi, as they are more commonly known, have a long and rich history despite the difficult conditions in which they live. A tribal proverb summarizes their existence quite simply: 'It is hard to be a Hopi, but it is good to be a Hopi.' Having occupied the three-mesa region since at least 500A.D., the Hopi have had to adapt to their harsh environment to survive. From their Anasazi ancestors, who emerged in the northern Southwest as early as 1500B.C., the Hopi learned to farm the inhospitable land. They became skilled at dry farming and built irrigated terraces along the mesa walls. From stone and mud they built their homes, and beneath the ground they constructed kivas for meetings and important religious ceremonies.

Religion, for the Hopis, was woven into every aspect of life. As author John D. Loftin noted in his book *Religion and the Hopi Life*, 'For them, work and ritual, practice and religion, are inseparably related.' The Hopi doctrine is filled with a myriad deities and spirits that connect them to their environment. And, although religious dances and ceremonies are performed exclusively by the men of the tribe, the importance of the feminine was not overlooked. A matrilineal people, the Hopi trace family and clan lineage through the female line as instructed by what is arguably their most important goddess, Spider Woman.

Like most oral traditions, it is difficult to determine which creation story is the 'correct' or oldest version. Variations are common and details have undoubtedly been lost or altered over time. Despite the discrepancies, Spider Woman remains at the heart of each story as a creator goddess and significant benefactor to the Hopi people. In the Hopi creation myths, of which we will explore two main variations, she plays an essential role in the creation and evolution of mankind. It is Spider Woman that both creates life and protects the worthy from destruction.

Spider Woman and Tawa

This version of the Hopi creation myth begins in a time when there were only two: Tawa the Sun God, and Spider Woman the Earth Goddess. Tawa ruled over the Above with all of its mysteries and power. The magic of the Below belonged to Spider Woman. They resided in the Underworld alone, without bird, beast, god or man.

Eventually the two decided that their labors were many and that helpers were needed to continue their work. Tawa split his essence in half and created Muiyinwuh, the God of All Life Germs. Spider Woman followed and split herself and created Huzruiwuhti, a goddess of turquoise, coral, silver, and other hard ornaments of wealth. Tawa took Huzruiwuhti as his wife and through their union the Magic Twins – Puukonhoya and Palunhoya – were born. As time crept on, from this union sprang Hicanavaiya, Man-Eagle, the Great Plumed Serpent, and a multitude of others. But still, their work felt unfinished.

Tawa and Spider Woman looked out upon the shimmering Endless Waters and had a mighty and magnificent Thought. They would create the Earth to lie between the realms of Above and Below. Sitting side by side in their turquoise-walled kiva, they began to sway their bodies and sing the first of many magic songs. The song wove together breeze and brook, life and light. Tawa sang, 'I am Tawa. I am Light. I am Life. I am Father of all that shall ever come.'

At his side, Spider Woman sang, 'I am Kokyanwuhti. I receive Light and nourish Life. I am Mother of all that shall ever come.' And into Tawa's mind, many thoughts began to take shape: birds to fly through the Above, beasts to graze upon the Earth, and fish to swim in the Waters. As he sang of the beautiful things he imagined, Spider Woman scooped up clay from the floor of the kiva and began to craft the Thoughts of Tawa. As she finished one, she lay it aside until she had crafted every Thought.

When she finished her work, Spider Woman and Tawa looked over their creations and saw that they did not breathe or move. Tawa then told Spider Woman, 'Each thing that has a form must also have a spirit, so now we must make a mighty magic.'

Over the lifeless clay figures, the god and goddess placed a woven blanket of fleecy wool. Tawa and Spider Woman then sang a powerful incantation, and the little figures began to spring to life beneath the blanket. But still their work was not finished.

Taking up the clay again, Spider Woman created two more figures. One she shaped into the likeness of Tawa. One she fashioned after her own shape. Again the blanket of creative wisdom was placed upon the figures and the magical words recited. However, this time, the figures remained lifeless. Spider Woman gathered the little figures to her breast, and the Sun God bent his eyes and will upon them. Together they began to sing the first Song of Life, giving breath and spirit to the newly formed humans.

Finally pleased with the work they had done, Tawa declared that he would create no more new life. But in order to nourish his creations, he would journey each day across the Above to shed his light upon them. Each night he would return to his wife in the Underworld, the realm of the first gods. Taking his blazing shield from the kiva wall, Tawa ascended into the Above, turned his fiery power to the Endless Waters, and created dry land for life to inhabit.

In the Below, Spider Woman gazed out lovingly at the throngs of creatures that crowded around her and began to separate them into groups. To each she gave a name, a place, and a purpose. Above the others she placed man and woman for they had been made in the likeness of the gods to rule over the lesser creatures. Through the Underworld she led them, until at last she came upon a sipapu, or opening, that led to the newly formed Earth. From the sipapu, she sent out the creatures and turned her attention to the man and woman. To the humans she established rules of proper living. Women, she declared, would build and care for the homes and nurture and teach the children. The men would build the kivas, stone structures underground where important religious ceremonies and clan meetings would take place. And although the family name would descend through the woman, it was man's job to provide sustenance and security to the family.

Promising man and woman a fertile land to sustain them, Spider Woman gave her last advice to her children. 'Have no fear, for we Two will be watching over you. Obey the words I have given you, and if you need help, call upon me.' With that, Spider Woman left the earth for the creatures and humans to multiply and fulfill their paths.

Spider Woman and Sótuknang

In many ways, the creation legend of Sótuknang and Spider Woman strongly resembles that of the Tawa story.

In this beginning, Tawa was alone in Tokpela, endless space. In the midst of the infinite void, Tawa began to plan how he wished for the universe to develop. To assist him with his purpose, Tawa created Sótuknang and called him his nephew. He gave Sótuknang the task of laying the foundations for the universe that he had designed. Sótuknang accepted the challenge and set out to manifest the desires of Tawa. He created land, water, and winds and placed them according to Tawa's will. Tawa looked out upon Sótuknang's progress and was pleased, but the nephew's work was not finished.

Tawa then instructed Sótuknang to fill the worlds he had created with life. Knowing that he would need assistance in this great task, Sótuknang first created Spider Woman as his helper. To her he gave the task of creating life to fill the world with joyful sound and movement. To Spider Woman he said, 'You have been given the knowledge, the wisdom, and the love to bless all the beings you create.' And so Spider Woman began to mold from the earth and her own saliva, all the creatures of earth. Each creature, and the very earth itself, were tuned to the voice of their creator, Tawa. The vibrations ran through all and created a world of sound, all in praise of the sun god.

Sótuknang was pleased with Spider Woman's creations and called to Tawa to come and behold the beautiful world they had created. Tawa was pleased and gave his final instruction – to create mankind to rule over the newly formed world and its creatures. From clays of red, white, yellow, and black, Spider Woman crafted woman in her image and man in the image of Sótuknang. She gave to the people language, purpose, and sent them out to their proper places. And she reminded them before she parted to remember her words, to always give thanks to Tawa for all they had been given, and to call upon her if they were in need.

Despite the differences in these two stories, the vital role of Spider Woman is evident. She is the earth mother, and it is through her that all life springs. But this is not the end of Spider Woman's role in the Hopi religion. The Hopi believe that we are currently living in the Fourth World, or Tuwaqachi. Each of the three worlds before the present was destroyed by Tawa when its human inhabitants began to forget the laws given to them by Spider Woman. Each time, however, Spider Woman would gather and protect all those that had kept to the proper path, leading them from the dying world into the new. Known as 'the great teacher,' Spider Woman taught her human children skills necessary for their survival and interceded between them and the deities.

Although undoubtedly the primary goddess of the Hopi people, Spider Woman is not the only female deity of importance. Also of great reverence among the Hopi are the kachinas, spirit beings that personify all things in the cosmos. There are kachinas that represent elements, weather, plants, and animals. Others are kachinas of locations, concepts, or even ancestors. Among them is Angwusnasomtaka, the Crow Mother, mother of all kachinas who leads the initiation rites for newborn Hopi children. Hahai-i Wuhti, whose name means 'pour water woman', is considered to be the grandmother of all kachinas. Her imagery is very similar to the Buddhist goddess, Kwan Yin. She is often depicted pouring water from a gourd symbolizing the way life was poured out onto the earth by Spider Woman. Ku'yapalitsa reigned over childbirth and the hunt while Kuwánlelenta personified and protected the sunflower plant. The kachina are as unlimited and varied as the natural world.

While most kachinas performed one specialized role in the tapestry of Hopi life, two female kachinas embodied particularly important aspects. The Butterfly Maiden was the kachina that governed the season of spring. From her wings she pollinated the plants necessary for the survival of the Hopi people. Through her magic, the Butterfly Maiden spread transformation and new beginnings on both a physical and spiritual level. The Hopi believed that she was also responsible for creating night-time dreams and for making those dreams come true. For the Hopi, like so many other peoples throughout history, the butterfly was a symbol of rebirth and regeneration.

In the stark Hopi homelands, corn was life. So it is no surprise that the Blue Corn Maiden was a kachina of special significance. Hopi legend speaks of a time when blue corn grew all year long thanks to the beautiful Blue Corn Maiden. She was a kind and gentle kachina that brought life and happiness to the people. But one day, while out gathering firewood, Blue Corn Maiden caught the attention of Winter Kachina. In a story very similar to that of the Greek Persephone and Hades, Winter Kachina stole Blue Corn Maiden and trapped her in his wintery home. Eventually, Blue Corn Maiden's friend Summer Kachina was able to rescue her from Winter Kachina. The two spirits came to an agreement that Blue Corn Maiden would remain with the Hopi people half of the year and with Winter Kachina the other half. In this way, Blue Corn Maiden not only became a symbol of spring and life, but also one of returning hope and the promise that after the winter had passed, the all-important corn would grow again.

The belief in kachinas demonstrates an important concept in Hopi religion: all things, both sentient and non-sentient, contain a unique and meaningful spirit. And since all spirit comes from the mother goddess Spider Woman, and the sun god Tawa, all things are sacred. From the sky above to the smallest grain of sand, each piece of creation is important and worthy of respect. The Hopis demonstrate their respect for the kachinas through their deep reverence for the earth and its inhabitants. While the remainder of the world is only beginning to understand the importance of conservation, the Hopi have been practicing it for centuries – not only for ecological reasons, but also because by doing so they honor their creators and give thanks for all they have been given. The lesson of the kachinas is a simple one. All of creation is a gift and deserves both respect and protection.

The lessons taught by Spider Woman are much more multi-faceted. It is believed that as she crafted all the creatures of the earth, Spider Woman connected to each a thin string of web. This string was attached to a 'door' on the top of each creature's head. Each string was also attached to the earth so that if a vibration ran through any one strand, the others would experience it too. Before she departed from the humans she had created, she advised them to 'keep the door opened' so that the word of their Creator could be heard. At the end of each of the previous worlds, the Hopi believe that humanity began to lose, or ignore, that connection. Eventually this turning away from the laws given by Spider Woman led to the destruction of the three worlds. The lessons here are obvious – keep an open mind and remember that all things share a connection. Life is a web of many strands, each affecting the others in some way. Actions have consequences, even if we don't notice them immediately. Spider Woman also reminds us that we share a connection with the earth itself and that we must learn to listen to what the natural world is whispering to each of us. To ignore that whisper is to tempt destruction.

For the Hopi, nothing is more important than following the path first laid out by Spider Woman. They honor her, and the other deities, in everything they do. There is no separation of religion and daily life. They are one in the same for each is a gift from the god and goddess. The Hopi way of life is difficult, but it must be that way. At the dawn of the fourth and present world, Spider Woman warned the people that an easy life would soon cause them to fall back into the evil ways that had caused the destruction of the previous worlds. The Hopi are grateful for the hardships they face for through them they honor the commandments of their creators. It is a beautiful concept: even the most difficult of times serve a greater purpose. The Hopi approach challenges with a heart of gratitude for the opportunity to grow and reconnect to the great web of life.

Today, Hopi life is an amalgamation of ancient beliefs and modern conveniences. And while technology and modernity are now common, the Hopi hold to their ancestral ways perhaps more than any other native tribe. Traditional ceremonies are still performed at auspicious times throughout the year. The stories and lessons of Spider Woman and the kachinas are still taught to Hopi children. The Hopi reverence for the spiritual essence of all things is still evident in all that they do. They remind us that life is a spiritual experience just as much as it is a physical one. In all that we do, we must remember to give thanks for both the blessings and challenges the spirits bestow upon us.

In recent years, as technology helped spread the stories of the Hopi, more and more people have found themselves drawn to the teachings of Spider Woman and the kachinas. Modern pagans who seek to reconnect to the great interconnected web of life seek out Spider Woman in new ways, calling on her for assistance just as she instructed the first peoples to do in times of need. Traditional kachina dolls are placed on altars as reminders of the divinity in all things. The locations and modes may change, but the heart of the Hopi religion remains. And it reaches through both time and space to remind others to approach all things with an open mind and a grateful heart.

Laurie Martin-Gardner is a reiki master-teacher, author, and artisan. Laurie is a lifelong student of myth and magick. She currently has two books available and frequently writes for several spiritual magazines.

Maya

The ancient Mayan empire spanned geographically from modern day El Salvador east to Honduras, north to Guatemala, east to Belize and north to the southern Mexican states of Chiapas, Tabasco, Yucatan, Quintana Roo and Campeche on the Yucatan Peninsula. During the height of the empire, the Classic Period, (250-900 A.D.), the population numbered in the millions.

The Mayan empire collapsed over time due to a number of factors: war, disease, environmental degradation and loss of faith in the ruling elite. However, the Maya did not 'disappear'. They simply moved away from the cities and created small hamlets and villages, many of which still exist today.

The Mayan realm was enormous. There were many factions among the Classic and Post Classic Period Maya and thus much aggression and warfare. Captives were taken, rulers assassinated. There were clearly strong cultural links, which made all the peoples Maya. But in terms of religion, the different groups had different goddesses in their pantheons. The Yucatec and K'iche' Maya groups were the largest and from what texts remain we can see numerous 'moon' goddesses who have similar traits and associations.

The Bishop Diego de Landa (12 November 1524-29 April 1579) from the Roman Catholic Archdiocese of Yucatan produced many writings on the pre-Columbian Maya and their culture, beliefs, myths etc. These documents are great sources for historians and archaeologists. But de Landa, in accordance with the Spanish Inquisition, conducted an auto de fe among the Maya. On July 12, 1562, more than 100 Mayan codices (bark books of which only four remain) and 5,000 Maya cult images were burned. In this single act, de Landa deprived not only the Maya of the time, but also their descendants of their own written history.

Among all the modern Maya peoples, the Yucatec Maya are

the largest and currently inhabit the Yucatan Peninsula and northern Belize. Modern speakers number close to 1.2 million as of the 2009 census. The Itza Mayan population lives in Guatemala in the Peten Region around Flores. There are very few fluent Itza speakers remaining as the language has all but vanished.

The K'iche' Maya live in the Guatemalan highlands and number about 1.5 million people. Other Mayan groups in the Guatemalan highlands include; the Achi, Akatek, Chuj, Ixil, Jakaltek, Kaqchikel, Mam, Poqomam, Poqomchi', Q'anjob'al', Tz'utujil and Uspantek.

The Lacandon Maya live in the Lacandon forest in Chiapas, Mexico. They are a small and insular group living very much the way their ancestors did. The Chiapas region is also home to other small Mayan groups; the Tzotzil, the Tzeltal and the Tojolabalis.

The culture among all of these groups have many similarities that make them distinctively Maya even though the words they speak are different enough to be distinct languages and not merely dialects. Their religion is more syncretistic, blending Mayan beliefs with Catholic ones.

What we know of ancient Mayan religion comes from epigraphic sources such as stelae, (stone monuments carved with glyphs and images in city centers), and codices (bark books containing written documents) as well as art and the *Popul Vu*, a western Guatemalan collection of myths and stories from the time. The Mayan pantheon comprised many, many gods, but only a few goddesses. The goddesses discussed here can be found in the *Books of Chilam Balam, Lacandon* and other cultural group ethnography, the *Madrid Codex*, the works of Diego de Landa, and the *Popol Vuh*. Depending on the source, most names are either Yucatec or K'iche', which are the two language families still widely spoken today among the Maya in Central America.

Ix Chel

One of the goddesses still spoken of today among the modern

Maya is Ix Chel. She is a moon, earth and rainbow goddess. She corresponds to Goddess O in the *Dresden Codex* (Taube, Karl, The Birth Vase: Natal Imagery in Ancient Maya Myth and Ritual. In Justin Kerr, ed., The Maya Vase Book: *A Corpus of Rollout Photographs of Maya Vases*, Volume 4. New York: Kerr Associates 1994.) Ix Chel is a patroness of weavers, the fiber arts, and pregnant women. She is the goddess of healing, medicine and for the Yucatec Maya she is the queen of life. She embodies the healing power that ancient cultures attributed to wise elder women. The rite of passage into womanhood for the Yucatec Maya required fashioning a clay image of Ixchel, traveling to her temple on the sacred Isle of Women (Isla Mujeres) and performing a ritualistic breaking of the image (Tozzer, Alfred, *Landa's Relación de las Cosas de Yucatán*, a Translation. 1941). There are a number of stories about Ix Chel. One of the best known myths is how she became the moon goddess.

Ix Chel's lover was the sun, Itzamna. This was against her grandfather's wishes and in anger, he cast a lightning bolt at Ix Chel and killed her. For 183 days, dragonflies sang over her body. On the final day, she awoke and fled to the sun's palace to be with her lover once more. The sun became jealous of Ix Chel, thinking she was having an affair with his brother, the morning star. Itzamna threw her out of heaven and then apologized, asking her to come back again. His mood constantly changed from loving to jealous rage and eventually Ix Chel had had enough. She escaped into the night and remained forever invisible when the sun was present. In her new home of the night, she spent her evenings nursing women of the Earth through their labor and the births of their children.

Ix Chel and Itzamna had 13 children and created the heavens and the earth and the beings who belong to it (Coe, Michael (1977). 'Supernatural Patrons of Maya Scribes and Artists,' in N. Hammond. *Social Process in Maya Prehistory*. Princeton, New Jersey: Princeton University Press. pp. 327-347.)

In another version, Ix Chel, called Po, is daughter of the Earth God. According to Eric Thompson, Po is wooed and finally captured by sun. They sleep together and are discovered by Po's father. The couple flees. Po's father is furious to have his daughter ruined. 'In all likelihood, this patriarchal punishment of a basic infraction of the rules of alliance represents the origin of menstruation, the 'evil blood' of a disobedient daughter colouring the water of sea and lake red, or sinking into the earth' (H.E.M. Braakhuis, *Xbalanque's Canoe. The Origin of Poison in Q'eqchi' – Mayan Hummingbird Myth.* Anthropos 100-1 (2005): 173-191). Po's menstrual blood is stored in thirteen jars. First the blood is transformed into many creatures such as snakes and insects. Thompson speculates this transformation is the origin of poison and the diseases causality. The thirteenth jar is the lunar jar: When it is opened, the moon is reborn from it.

Awilix

Awilix was a Postclassical Period (1000-1697A.D.) goddess among the highland Guatemalan K'iche' Maya. She was also considered a moon goddess and was probably derived from the Classic Period Ix Chel. She is associated with the Underworld, death, sickness and was the patroness of the Ballgame. Awilix is one of a trinity of gods for the K'iche' Maya, called the Tohil, and was the most important of them. (Christenshon, Allen J. (2003, 2007). 'Popul Vuh: Sacred Book of the Quiché Maya People' (PDF online publication). *Mesoweb articles.* Mesoweb: An Exploration of Mesoamerican Cultures. Retrieved 2010-02-17.)

Ixtab

According to Diego de Landa, Ixtab, Rope Woman is the goddess of suicides. In Yucatec society, suicide by hanging was considered an honorable way to die under certain circumstances. Ixtab accompanies such dead along with women who die in childbirth and men who died as soldiers and those who died as sacrificial tributes, to the underworld. There the dead will lounge under a Yaxche tree and eat wonderful food and drink, spending eternity in paradise. She is pictured as a dead woman with a rope around her neck and a decaying body in the *Dresden Codex* (J.E.S. Thompson, *A Commentary on the Dresden Codex*. Philadelphia 1972).

Xquic

Xquic, in English Blood Mood or Blood Maiden/Goddess, is a K'iche' Maya goddess from the 16th century. She's talked about in the Popul Vu. She was the daughter of one of the lords of *Xibalba*, the Mayan Underworld, called Cuchumaquic, and is the mother of the Hero Twins from the *Popul Vu*, Hunahpu and Xbalanque.

As told in the Popul Vu, Xquic went to investigate a calabash tree where the Lords of Xibalba had displayed the severed head of the god Hun Hunahpu, whom they had sacrificed. The calabash bore a strange fruit resembling a human skull. As she reached for the fruit, the skull spat on her hand causing her to become pregnant with the twins.

After six months her pregnancy became obvious and she was questioned by the Lords of Xibalba regarding the father. She claimed not to know the face, as the skull did not truly have a face, and the fetuses were declared to be bastards. Xquic was sentenced to exile.

Xquic sought the protection of Xmucane, the mother of Hun Hunahpu and after several tests to prove who she was and that she was indeed carrying the twins of Xmucane's dead son, she was welcomed into the household where the twins were later born.

There are a few other Mayan goddesses from various periods and language groups that have very little written about them. There are slight descriptions in the *Popul Vu* and some of these descriptions come from modern-day Mayan verbal histories.

Colel Cab

Goddess of the Bees. Bees, like bats, were highly revered creatures among the Maya.

Ixazaluoh

The goddess of water and weaving.

Akna

A motherhood and birthing goddess associated with the moon and the Bacabs. These are the four gods who stand at the four corners of the world and hold up the heavens.

Mayahuel

The goddess who discovered pulque, a fermented drink used in ceremony and a precursor to modern tequila. She is a Lacandon Maya goddess.

Xpuch and Xtah

Another tale from the *Popul Vu* speaks of Xpuch and Xtah, two maidens of the Vuc Amag tribe who were forced to offer themselves to the gods Tohil, Avilix and Hacavitz. These gods promised to leave the tribe unmolested if the maidens returned with proof they had been violated by the gods.

There are still modern goddess cults among the Maya. The most well-known being the Cult of Ix Chel. 'Considering that 500 years have elapsed since the Spanish Conquest,' says Harvard University ethnologist Evon Z. Vogt, 'I am impressed with the enduring nature of Classic Maya religious concepts and beliefs.' Additionally, there are cross-over beliefs between the Maya and other past and present Mesoamerican cultures. Again, using Ix Chel as an example, in some representations of her, an entwined serpent serves as Ix Chel's headdress, crossed bones often adorn her skirt, and instead of human hands and feet, she sometimes has claws. One can see very similar features in representations of the Aztec earth goddesses, Tlaltecuhtli, Tocî, and Cihuacoatl.

De Landa writes of a 16th century cult of Ix Chel in which Maya women who were hopeful of a fruitful marriage would travel to the sanctuary of Ix Chel on the island of Cozumel. According to de Landa, Cozumel was the most important place of pilgrimage after Chichen Itza (which was an Aztec site, not a Mayan one), off the east coast of the Yucatan peninsula. The women would seek out a priest who lay hidden in a large stelae and acted as an oracle, foretelling their future.

Many of these women would then travel to a small island north of Cozumel, Isla Mujeres (the Isle of Women). The island was named by Hernandez de Cordoba because of the multitude of female stone idols he found there dedicated to Ix Chel, Ixchebeliax, Ixhunie and Ixhunieta. These idols were '...only vestured from the girdle down, and having the breast covered after the manner of the Indians' (de Landa).

On the western side of the Yucatan peninsula, Acalan, the main town in Chontal province venerated Ixchel as one its main deities. Hernan Cortés describes a special location in Acalan where unmarried young women were sacrificed to a 'goddess in whom they put great trust and hope,' possibly again Ix Chel (Scholes, France V., and Ralph L. Roys, *The Maya Chontal Indians of Acalan-Tixchel*. Norman: University of Oklahoma Press 1968).

The history and prehistory of the goddesses of the Mayan pantheon stretches back to pre-Columbia times, as far back as the first millennium BC or earlier. Modern Maya practice a religion that weaves both native and Catholic ideas together, even referring to Christ as the Sun God and Mary as the Moon Goddess. The Maya see no difficulty in this and for most Maya, their religion and beliefs are deeply rooted in their way of life. Most modern Maya still live in closed communities and practice the old ways, farm as they always have, rely on midwives and healers as opposed to modern Western medicine, and worship much as they always have. In the Classic Period, the elite rulers were the ones who spoke to the gods for the people. Today, it is the village mayor (alcalde), even though the priest is the religious leader. The Mayan people and their culture are resilient. They've faced the collapse of their culture many times over the millennia from within and without. Western scholars have been studying them for well over one hundred years and we still have so much to learn. The Mayan pantheon of gods and goddess is rich and diverse, well worth our study.

Heather L Marano is a writer and Mayan scholar. She has published numerous articles on the Maya and has written a chapter in the Moon Books publication *Naming the Goddess*.

Part 2

The Migrant Goddess

The American Dilemma: Engaging in Non-Appropriative Pagan Practice

Goddess Worshipers and Pagans in America are faced with unique challenges when they feel drawn to practice a culturally specific spiritual path, or called to build relationships with divinities from a culture that differs from their own. Setting aside the complex and painful issues of colonialism for the moment, the United States is a nation of immigrants, and many American Pagans – especially those whose families migrated from Europe generations ago – are too far removed from their culture of origin to have direct connections to the homeland of their heritage or its people. To further complicate matters, many Americans are also of multicultural descent, resulting in the lack of a clear tether to bind them strongly to any one cultural heritage. Some Americans descend from families that have been in the United States for so long that they identify purely as Americans, and while they may feel no tie to the countries their families originally immigrated from, they are also left without a cultural connection to an ancestral spiritual practice; this leaves them with the options of either creating new traditions that connect them with the spirit of the land they live on, or seeking inspiration from indigenous American practices and beliefs.

These issues leave many American Pagans of immigrant descent caught between a rock and a hard place when it comes to cultural appropriation: they are often not connected enough to the cultural heritage of their blood lineage to be able to fully participate in its traditions, nor is there an easy way for them to connect to the authentic traditions of the land where they live. Further, even should they seek to work with the divinities with whom they share a blood heritage connection, there can sometimes be friction with practitioners who do still dwell in the cultural homeland, who sometimes see these American seekers as alien while believing that one needs to live in the divinities' place of origin in order to fully understand them or participate in their worship.

In contrast, should non-Native Americans turn to the divinities and spirits of the land where they live, they are confronted with very real issues of being either the direct descendants of those who took this land from First Nations peoples, or else being part of the overarching American culture that continues to marginalize and disempower Native American peoples today, even if they personally play no part in such injustices. Surely there is no easy way to gain entry into indigenous folkways when the colonization of the New World by Europeans was accomplished through spilled blood and great suffering; and truly, should there not be *something* that remains wholly in the hands of Native American peoples? The many tribes and nations of North America have rich cultural diversity, and an investment in keeping their spiritual practices and sacred traditions within the confines of their own people is completely understandable, especially in the face of very real attempts to appropriate these practices by exploitative teachers derisively termed 'Plastic Shamans.'

Finally, in the multicultural realities of our world, there are Pagans who feel called to work with divinities and in traditions whose cultures of origin differ from their own blood heritage; this can be perceived as another iteration of appropriation even when the seeker is of European descent interested in European traditions that originate in cultures other than their own. These issues leave us with several threads of inquiry to explore: is the ability to participate in traditional folkways connected to cultural practice or genetic bloodlines, and how does one define 'homeland' when it comes to spirituality – is one's spiritual home where one lives, where one's blood heritage originates, or can it be something that calls from outside of claims of dwelling or lineage?

These are complicated issues, to be sure, and there are ongoing discussions about these issues in modern Paganism, especially surrounding sensitivity to appropriation of traditions from historically exploited cultures, as well as concerns over calls for racial purity in some fringe elements of Norse and Celtic Neopaganism. For myself, I tend to look to the past to see how our ancestors processed these matters. In some cases, it appears that the Gods of old were not static; they tended to travel along with their people, and through the physical movement of populations or the transmission of ideas from one place to another, some Gods transcended cultural and geographic boundaries. The Romans, for example, avidly worshiped divinities from other lands side by side with their own Gods. The worship of Isis was incredibly popular in the Roman Empire, their military contained many followers of Mithraism – a mystery religion originating in Persia – and many in the Roman cavalry held great devotion for Epona, a Goddess from Celtic Gaul.

In addition to the major Gods of their cultures, what we would call their main pantheon today, many in the ancient world also worshiped local divinities; these could be deified ancestors connected to their family lineages, genus loci connected to natural phenomenon such as landscape features, or minor Gods holding patronage over smaller tribal or kinship groups in specific locales. These latter divinities were more connected to specific places and particular peoples, and likely did not receive much worship outside of these more limited spheres of influence. In Celtic Gaul, Miranda Green writes, the names of more than 400 different Celtic gods are found on inscriptions from the Roman period on, and of these, 300 appear just once. The more localized distributions may point to tribal divinities or those who were genius loci of a particular location, while more widespread mentions could indicate a more universal Celtic pantheon of sorts.

These examples show that in ancient Europe there were

divinities that were specific to a people and a landscape, as well as those whose worship was taken up by those outside of their culture and place of origin. As modern-day participants in the western civilization that has its roots in old Europe, Americans have a strong cultural connection to the divinities of the Old World, even if they themselves are not of European descent. Because of this, I believe that if approached with proper respect, and with sensitivity towards issues of appropriation, American Pagans can develop meaningful religious practices centering on the Goddesses and Gods of Europe if they feel drawn to work with them; there is ancient precedent for long-standing worship of these divinities by foreign peoples and in foreign lands. As a first generation American of Italian descent, I feel more comfortable with this in terms of indigenous European folkways rather than those traditions that originate in the East or come from cultures that have been historically co-opted and colonized by Europeans; I feel those cultures must speak for themselves when it comes to their positions on outsiders participating in their spiritual traditions.

Philosophy of Engagement

Over the years, I developed a philosophy of engagement as a way to approach and build relationships with divinities, especially with those who arise from, or are connected to, different lands than those where we dwell and who may also be outside of our own cultural paradigm. I believe it to be a guideline to help the seeker forge connections and come into right relationship with divinities while also avoiding issues of cultural appropriation or risking removing them from the textured complexities of their cultural context. Keep in mind that these are offered as a guide, and that you need not adopt all of these suggestions into your practice. Some of the points may call to you more than others, while others may not be possible for you at the present time; I believe that the intention to be respectful, a willingness to learn, and an open heart provide the necessary foundation to engage in a culturally specific practice.

1: Listen

There are many different ways to listen. Listen to your heart, and honor the call that you may be feeling to connect with a certain Goddess, especially if it is coming from an unexpected source. Listen to those who are members of the culture from which you are drawing spiritual inspiration; this is a key skill, which can help prevent you from causing an unintentional offense as well as leave you open for opportunities to receive shared first-hand knowledge and insight. If you are seeking to engage with a Goddess who originates in a still-living culture, even if that culture does not actively worship her, it is especially important for you to listen, particularly when seeking to understand a viewpoint or sociocultural experience that differs from your own. Do not try to define a cultural experience for others, nor overlay your own expectations over their realities. It is my experience, for example, that the Welsh are very connected to the legends of their people, and while they may not be Pagan nor even view some of the mythological personages in their tales as divinities, they are aware of the stories that have been woven through the landscape of their country. If you take the time to listen, you may find gems of folk practice and tradition you would otherwise have never learned. Be open. Listen.

2: Engage in Culture

Culture is not a matter of genetics or bloodline; culture is a verb, and it something that you must do, rather than something you are. To become actively engaged in a culture accomplishes several things: it helps preserve traditions and transmit cultural wisdoms; it provides insight into the people who birthed, developed, and maintained traditions over time; when approached respectfully, it is a way to honor the culture and its people, especially when doing so helps to support and preserve aspects of the culture; and, from a spiritual perspective, it can deepen your understanding of the divinities with whom you are seeking to build relationships because culture gives context.

There are many ways to practice culture. Language is the primary mode of cultural transmission, and so to really under-stand a culture, studying its language is a powerful way to become a participant. In places where the old tongues have been repressed or are in danger of dying out, learning the language not only shows deep respect to those who are native speakers, but also provides you with an opportunity to give something back to the culture by helping to keep the language alive. Even if language is not your gift or area of interest, knowing how to correctly pronounce Goddess names and places from myths, or to recite prayers and invocations in the language of origin is a powerful way to honor your divinities. To be sure, the Goddesses and Gods understand that which is in our hearts, and so language is ultimately not a limitation when it comes to connecting with the divine – Athena does not only understand ancient Greek, for example. Yet, if we meditate on the fact that many ancient cultures considered words and writing to be sacred, certainly there are deeper mysteries at play when it comes to the importance of language.

Another way to engage in culture is to learn and practice traditional crafts and art forms, which include music, dance, folk costume, poetry, textile making, artisan crafts, fine arts, and even cuisine. Study the culture's history. Read the primary sources for its myths, legends, and folklore. Join a cultural society or take some classes at a local university. Immersing yourself in some aspect of their culture of origin is a powerful way to understand and begin to develop relationships with divinities to whom you feel drawn, but with whom you do not share common folkways.

Finally, when drawing religious inspiration from the divinities of a living culture, I believe it is important to ensure that you are not just taking and using without giving anything back. Cultural appropriation is a hurtful practice in which many otherwise well-meaning people unconsciously participate. Be sure that you are mindful of cultural and historical context, that you are not just using a thin veneer of cultural symbols and forms to give a certain flavor to your otherwise foreign practice, and that you actively support the culture by giving back in some way. This exchange can take the form of making donations to museums, trusts, and organizations that maintain important sites and cultural artifacts related to your pantheon; immersing yourself in learning, and then teaching others about the culture of origin of your deities; and volunteering your time or giving monetary support to cultural activities that transmit and preserve folkways, be they local Greek festivals or online archives of ancient documents.

3: Emulate Practice

In my opinion, one of the best ways to honor a divinity is to craft a practice which – when possible – mirrors traditional ritual forms, uses authentic prayers and chants, and incorporates symbols and offerings that our spiritual forebears used as part of their worship. While intention, love, and spiritual openness are of course at the heart of any practice or worship, incorporating aspects of the way the original worshipers of the Goddesses and Gods approached them permits you to travel a well-worn path of connection – one birthed and developed within the same cultural context as the divinities themselves. This is not to say that modern iterations of practice are dishonoring. Rather, when you are reaching out to forge a relationship with a divinity, it is a powerful thing to express your desire to connect with and honor them by demonstrating that you are learning all you can about them and are putting this knowledge into practice. For example, when creating ritual for a Goddess, gift her with the types of offerings she was historically given, burn an incense blend you created based on old temple recipes or else made of flowers native to her land, offer up chants and prayers created for her that have passed through the lips of worshipers for hundreds or thousands of years, or else create new praise songs that incorporate the lore and symbolism associated with the Goddess with whom you seek to enter into relationship.

Certainly, human relationships with divinities are not unchanging, and the ways to honor the Goddesses and Gods in their cultures of origins evolved over time and as their worship grew outside of the bounds of their original culture. There is room for growth and space for change in every practice, to be sure, but having your starting point be one that is grounded in fact by conducting a thorough review of history, archaeology, and primary source mythology, will serve you well in developing a strong relationship with the divine.

Reconstructionism is not a path that appeals to everyone, but I have found that doing your best to incorporate elements of authentic practice in your work will open up doors of deep connection, because you are tying into a well-established energetic pathway empowered by the intentions built by centuries of worshipers – crossing an already-constructed bridge, if you will – rather than having to build an entirely new one from scratch. Remember, too, that like energies attract. The more your shrine, altar, or ceremony reflects the energy and culture of the divinities you are working with, the easier it will be to connect to them. Once these symbolic and energetic keys are in place and the door to relationship has been opened, you can refine your work and inner process with direct influence from the divine.

4: Connect with the Land

While it is my belief and experience that Goddesses and Gods are not limited to particular times or physical locations, I do feel that places associated with their worship as well as landscape areas connected to their mythos are places of power that can facilitate the connections we seek to forge with our divinities – especially when one lives an ocean away. It is one thing to read the lore of the Goddesses and Gods with whom you work, yet something else entirely to stand within their mythic landscapes, completely immersed in ancient energies and obtaining an understanding of how a particular place holds such a deep and powerful connection with divinity. While it is not always possible to do so, making a pilgrimage to visit sites sacred to the Goddesses you work with is a once-in-a-lifetime experience that can forever enrich your relationships with the divine.

While the act of pilgrimage is an incredible outward expression of devotion, often involving sacrifice and hardship to gather the resources that will permit you to make the physical journey, there are other ways you can connect with sacred sites. Using images of place as a focus for meditation is an excellent tool for connection, as is working with waters or conscientiously gathered objects – such as a pendant charged in the landscape, a small clod of earth, or a pressed flower – which others have brought back with them from the site. Please keep in mind that while in some places, such as at holy wells, collecting waters is encouraged; however, at others, taking a small token to connect one to the landscape must be done in the most honoring way possible, if at all. You cannot take a piece of a stone circle, for example, but certainly you can bring your own crystal to the site to be charged on one of the stones in order to bring the energies of place back with you. Be conscientious of what an area can bear: taking a stone from a pebble beach does not have the impact that stripping the leaves from a hawthorn tree does. When it comes to flora, I prefer to gather what has already fallen, or else make energetic elixirs from still-living plants that grow in and around the sacred sites I visit; the energies come home with me, while the plants remain whole and healthy.

Similarly, a powerful way to make a connection to place is by leaving an offering, but these too should be chosen with care. Do not leave behind anything that is not biodegradable or will leave the site cluttered for those who come after you. I have found that pouring libations out to honor the area, and gifting small charged stones to running waters to be the best kind of offerings. In Celtic lands, the tradition of tying a cloutie or prayer ribbon near holy wells is alive and well, and many sites are beautifully festooned with colored fabrics dancing in the wind. Again, be aware of local tradition and remember that sacred sites are not there for you to plunder or deface; you are a guest in these places and they should be treated with the utmost care and respect, both to honor the land as well as its associated spirits and divinities.

Conclusion

American Pagans of immigrant descent are often in a position to have to navigate difficult waters when it comes to following a culturally specific spiritual tradition. Issues of cultural appropriation arise both when they seek to participate in the indigenous folkways of their ancestral heritage originating across an ocean, as well as with those tied to the land where they were born and dwell. While there is no simple solution, there has to be a middle ground solution, and I believe that answer lies in participation in a culture – giving back to the peoples from whom one draws spiritual inspiration by respecting their traditions, learning their ways, and helping to preserve the culture by participating in some aspect of it. One's blood or DNA, in my opinion, is less important than how one actively engages with the culture, tradition, and societal mores of the nations from which one's Goddesses arise. In the end, one's spiritual homeland is found nowhere but within one's own heart, and the route to creating that connection with the inner divine that is traveled by engaging in a respectful and informed culturally traditional practice can be a rich experience indeed.

Jhenah Telyndru holds a masters degree in Celtic Studies from the University of Wales, Trinity Saint David. She is the founder of the Sisterhood of Avalon, and her published works include *Avalon Within: A Sacred Journey of Myth, Mystery, and Inner Wisdom*. Jhenah welcomes your contact through her website: www.ynysafallon.com.

Goddesses of Ireland: Beyond the Ninth Wave

It is a hotly debated topic in Irish and more generally Celtic paganism as to whether the Irish Gods travel with the people who worship them or whether they are sedentary, bound to specific places. People in favor of the latter view point out that the Irish Gods are strongly associated with specific locations in Ireland and that they are said in some cases to be embodied by the land, such as the hills called the Paps of Anu. This line of thought says that if the Gods are so strongly connected to those places then they cannot also be elsewhere. On the other hand there are those, myself included, who believe that the Gods know no geographic limits and can be found anywhere, especially where the people who worship them can be found. For the Irish Gods this would include not only Ireland, but also the Irish diaspora in Canada, Australia, and the United States, as well as anywhere else their names are spoken in reverence.

It is true that many if not all of the Irish Gods are said to have homes, or sidhe, in specific places. These were established when the Gods moved beneath the hills after the Milesians came and we know what many of them are because of the strong local folk traditions surrounding each location. The Tuatha Dé Danann are inextricably linked to real world places and these places are woven into the tapestry of the Gods' stories. Oweynagat is the Morrigan's and part of the story of Odras. Brugh na Boyne is Oengus mac Og's and part of the story of his conception and cleverness, and is also associated with his mother, the Goddess Boann. Emhain Macha, also called Navan fort, is Macha's and a symbol of her sovereignty. Knockainey belongs to the Goddess Aine and likewise Cnoc Greine belongs to the Goddess Grian. The Irish Gods do not essentially live in some distant, unreachable world or some separate plane of existence; they live here, in our world, or at least their homes have physical, tangible, counterparts here that we can visit and see and touch. Perhaps this is what leads to a feeling that these places are not just where we can find the Gods living, but are the only places the Gods can be. However, if we look at myth we will see that our ancestors never held such a view. Each deity had many homes, many places, and some gained and lost different places over time, indicating the transient nature of these connections.

The Irish Gods, the Tuatha Dé Danann, were not native to Ireland, but rather came there later, whether you choose to believe that in the mythic sense outlined by the Invasion Cycle or whether you see them arriving with the Celtic culture. In the *Lebor Gabala Erenn* we find the story of Tuatha Dé Danann arriving in ships, either on the sea or from the sky, and fighting the beings who had already laid claim to Ireland in order to find a place there. In Celtic academia there are different theories about the way that pan-Celtic deities (those found in several Celtic cultures) arrived in Ireland and came to be worshiped there. In either case they were foreign Gods once who made homes in a new place. We see echoes of this ability to go where the people honoring them went in the spread of the worship of the Gaulish goddess Epona to Rome, as her worship caught on with Roman soldiers and was imported back to their homes. We see this as well in the way that the Irish migrating to Scotland brought with them some of their Gods, including Brighid and Angus and possibly the Cailleach. The Gods are not omniscient or omnipotent, but they are Gods and it is entirely within their ability to go where they will, if they are being called and honored in a new place. Even the slua sidhe, the fairy host, is said to be able to cross the ocean and journey far afield of their homes; why would the Gods be able to do any less?

There are several examples of specific Irish Goddesses who are active in America, both in that they have many worshipers here and in having had groups founded or dedicated to them here. These Goddesses are some of the more well-known and also most loved, and while they each have their own sacred sites in Ireland they also have found a place in a new land. Among these are Brighid, the Morrigan, and Danu.

Brighid is certainly one of the most popular and well known Irish Goddesses in America. In recent years more Americans are writing about this powerful Goddess, reclaiming her ancient pre-Christian roots while exploring who she is to them as Irish-Americans or Americans. They speak of her history and her deep roots in Ireland, of her sacred places there and the way her story weaves into that of the Catholic Saint Brigid, but they also speak of modern experiences with Brighid outside of Ireland. Brighid is, like most Irish deities, a mystery to be explored, a single deity and a triplicity, as well as other related Brighids who may or may not be the same. The name Brighid, which appears alternatively as Brig, Bric, and Brigit, is both a title and a name, and *Cormac's Glossary* tells us that the name is used as a synonym for 'goddess'. Brighid appears as a daughter of the Dagda, as a poet, as a healer, as a smith, as a judge, and in association with outlaws, hinting at her complex character. In modern America we can find all of these Brighids being honored, sometimes separately and sometimes seen as a single deity. Because of her widespread popularity she is honored by a wide variety of different pagans, from traditional witches to Irish Reconstructionist Polytheists, from modern Druids to eclectic pagans. All across America Brighid is honored on her special holiday of Imbolc by people who may not consider themselves Irish or even Celtic pagans.

In Kildare, Ireland, there is a shrine to Brighid with a perpetual flame tended by nuns. This practice was adopted by pagans as well during the 1990s in the Americas, specifically Canada, where a group called Daughters of the Flame began flame-tending for the Goddess; later the Ord Brighideach was founded as well for the same purpose, although it allowed men where the first group did not. I know many people in America who honor this Goddess and some who choose to do so by flame-tending. At the festival site of Brushwood in New York there is a permanent ritual site and at that site is a shrine for Brighid where people may leave offerings and pray. I have personally experienced the presence of Brighid in ritual in America many times, including once at a public ritual where a candle burned out and then several minutes later during a chant to Brighid spontaneously re-lit.

Another popular Irish Goddess in America is the Morrigan. There have been several books on her written by Americans, exploring a variety of viewpoints and understandings of her. Unlike Brighid, who has a fairly homogenous persona, the understanding of the Morrigan is enormously varied in ways that are often contradictory. Particularly, in my experience, among Americans we can find a huge array of different perceptions of the Morrigan, so much so that one person or group's view of her may be entirely at odds with another's. To some she is a single Goddess, to others a triple deity, occasionally envisioned as a neo-pagan Maiden-Mother-Crone, while to others she may encompass many other Irish Goddesses. Who she is and what other names she goes by is a fluid thing, but what is certain is that she moves strongly in America. More and more individuals feel called by her and several groups across the country are dedicated to her especially. She does have a somewhat fearsome reputation, and rightly so, and for many years in my experience, people would be cautioned not to honor her or call on her, but this trend is eroding as she gains popularity. Within the past few years especially there has been a boom in her worship with more and more pagans in America acknowledging and honoring the Morrigan. Public rituals are held to her at major events and spiritual retreats dedicated to her occur on American soil, inviting the presence of the Goddess to find a home in a new place.

Once seen mostly as a Goddess of soldiers, and one that books would warn people away from, the Morrigan in America has become as diverse and complex as those who worship her, encompassing everything from a fierce battle Goddess to a gentle mother Goddess. While some people do build an understanding of her through mythology and folklore many rely only on personal opinions, creating a dizzying array of ideas about her. There are several larger groups dedicated to her based in America, two of which run public rituals, retreats, and sacred pilgrimages to Ireland in her honor. There are also a countless number of smaller groups and individuals dedicated to her, although unlike the worship of Brighid, honoring the Morrigan seems less homogenous. I am not aware yet of any permanent public shrines to her, but as with the one for Brighid in New York I believe it is only a matter of time before one is created. In 2014 I was privileged to attend a retreat in her honor and was able to see firsthand the diversity of people who are being drawn to her worship and service, which included witches, Wiccans, Druids, and Reconstructionists, as well as those who choose no label beyond pagan. I myself have experienced the Morrigan, as Morrigu and by her other names of Badb and Macha, many times in America, in rituals dedicated to her and spontaneously. In one ritual at Brushwood, conducted by the Druid organization Ar nDraiocht Fein, when the Morrigan was called into the rite the temperature dropped noticeably to the point that people could see their breath in the air, which lasted for several minutes.

Another often mentioned Irish Goddess in America is Danu, one of the most obscure and intriguing of the Irish Goddesses. We know very little from ancient myth about this Goddess who is often credited as being the progenitor of the Irish Gods. Modern myths and stories are being created to fill the gaps and many people who feel drawn to her are also filling the empty spaces with their own personal experiences. Since the 1990s stories have also appeared in print telling new myths of Danu, such as Peter Berresford Ellis's imagined creation myth and

Alexei Kondratiev's article reconstructing Danu and Bile as possible progenitor deities. With the advent of blogging there has also been an increase in people sharing personal experiences and stories of Danu using that medium. As with the Morrigan I am not aware of any existing shrines to Danu in the Americas as of yet, but given her growing popularity it is also only a matter of time.

Additionally, there are many other Irish Goddesses who have found a home in the Americas, some more easily found in myth, some impossibly obscure. I have personally experienced Aine, Airmed, and Flidais while living in America. Flidais in particular came through with a very strong presence for me in a time of great personal stress, not when I was calling on her but spontaneously. I had honored her before and had some connection to her, but at the time I felt her in this way I was actually praying to another deity; however, it was Flidais who answered. This may demonstrate that while the Irish Goddesses are at home in Ireland they have the agency and ability to go wherever they choose, when they choose. These other Goddesses, like the more popular ones, are seen in different ways by those who honor them. Aine na gClair is known in America, but so is Aine as a goddess of the moon. The Cailleach, who is known in Cork, is also called on in America, but the understanding of her here often differs, with a greater emphasis on her only as a Goddess of winter and storms. The Irish Goddesses in America are often understood more strongly through the lens of personal belief and inspiration than history and myth, as so many here come to them divorced from Irish culture.

In America there is less – or often no – emphasis on each Irish Goddesses connection to physical places; their mythology is not grounded in tangible locations that can be visited and touched. Rather Irish Goddesses in America are rooted in the hearts of their worshipers, they are carried on the lips of those who honor them to new locations, new territory. And finding homes in these new places they flourish. The old traditions of honoring them go with them, sometimes kept as they have always been, sometimes adapted to different climates and perceptions. But as their worship grows here it may be that, like the shrine to Brighid at the festival site of Brushwood in New York, new sacred places and sacred sites will become known. It may be that the Irish Goddesses will lay claim to new territory by claiming new sacred sites, just as we see new stories being told of them.

Honoring the Irish Goddesses in the Americas does present certain challenges and require flexibility. Offerings to the Morrigan can be given to a bog, or swamp, in Ireland or America, but in a place with no crows or ravens, what birds can her followers look to as representing her? What new forms does she take in foreign places, where her traditional forms are unknown? For those who seek to honor Danu, a Goddess associated with rivers, how can that be done in the desert or other extremely dry places? For some people who live in areas that are fairly similar in climate to Ireland these questions are non-issues, but for others they are vital to spiritual practice. For the Irish Goddesses, who were always so closely tied to the land and things related to the land, creating a strong connection to the place where they are now honored is essential. In areas without crows or ravens, some people have turned to vultures as symbols of the Morrigan while others look to falcons. In dry places like the desert those seeking Danu may choose to honor the life-giving symbolism of water, all the more powerful where water is a rare and precious commodity.

When we move from place to place we bring our Gods with us because the Gods follow their people. Our relationship to them is symbiotic. We carry them with our traditions and practices and beliefs into new territories and new opportunities. In a way – perhaps the most important way – we ourselves are what anchor our Gods in this world as they migrate with us, until they establish new physical ties to things less transient. As paganism has found a place in America, so have the Irish Goddesses, following where those who worship them go, and as long as there are pagans in America worshipping them, the Irish Goddesses will be there.

Morgan Daimler is a blogger, poet, teacher of esoteric subjects, Druid, dedicant of Macha, and wandering priestess of Odin. She is the author of *Where the Hawthorn Grows* and the Pagan Portals books *Fairy Witchcraft, The Morrigan, Irish Paganism, Brigid* and *Fairycraft*. She lives in Connecticut, USA.

African Goddesses and Creole Voodoo

Syncretization is the identification of deities from one religious practice with those of another religious practice. Louisiana Voodoo is a religious and spiritual practice originating from the traditions of the African diaspora. It is a cultural form of the African-American religions that developed with the blending of the French, Spanish, and Creole-speaking African-American population of the U.S. state of Louisiana. These magickal practices are an amalgamation of western African religious and spiritual customs blended with European/American Christian religious customs by the African diaspora that were brought to America during the Trans-Atlantic Slave Trade. The slaves first arrived in New Orleans, Louisiana, in 1719 directly from western Africa. Throughout the 1700 and 1800s, thousands of western African peoples from Yoruba, Dahomey (now Benin), Bini, Ewe, and Fon were enslaved and brought to the Americas.

Louisiana Voodoo is often confused with, although it is not entirely divisible from, Haitian Vodou and southern Hoodoo. It differs from Vodou in its emphasis upon gris-gris (amulets or talismans), voodoo queens, use of Hoodoo occult paraphernalia, and Li Grand Zombi (a snake deity). It was through Louisiana Voodoo that such terms as 'gris-gris' and 'voodoo dolls' were introduced into the wider American culture. Louisiana Voodoo is about healing and community through contact with the loa (goddesses and gods) and ancestor veneration.

The slaves who were stolen from their native lands in Africa brought with them their beliefs and regional practices. Their owners or 'masters' did not recognize the spiritual qualities of their native ceremonies; instead they considered the Africans to be barbarians and, therefore, incapable of forming the abstract concepts necessary for spiritual practices. In the face of the horrific conditions of their enslavement, the Africans' only hope rested in their faith. Amid families and tribes being broken apart, they surely found unity and solace in their familiar ancient rituals. It almost certainly gave them a profound sense of inner freedom and strength. Worship had a profound influence upon the development of new religions such as Voodoo.

The word 'vodou' means 'spirit' in the Fon language of the people of Dahomey kingdom of western Africa. Along with their knowledge of herbs and their practice of creating talismans and amulets for use in spell work and healing, the worship of goddesses and gods was part and parcel of the culture the Africans brought with them to the New World.

One of the key factors that kept the African peoples' beliefs from extinction were the similarities between Voodoo and Catholicism. In areas where the majority religion of the local population was Catholicism, the slaves and their descendants often had to conceal the worship of their African goddesses and gods behind the façade of Catholic Church saints. Many practitioners who syncretized traditional Catholic Christianity with worship of the African deities often kept statuary of Catholic saints whom they believed corresponded with the various Voodoo deities on their home altars. As a result of the slave trade, the social and cultural environments of America saw worship of the traditional African deities undergo some subtle yet significant changes as they became syncretized with Catholicism and the French culture of south Louisiana. Various African rites and rituals, witchcraft and healing practices were incorporated into the Voodoo that developed in Louisiana. This adaptation was necessary for the African slaves and their descendants in their practice of Voodoo in order to avoid persecution. This is one of many American manifestations of Vo-dun religions with its roots in the Dahomey kingdom of West Africa.

Ancestor worship also is an integral aspect of Louisiana Voodoo. The veneration of ancestors and the resultant emphasis on respect for elders is another aspect of Louisiana Voodoo brought from western Africa. This spiritual and cultural practice resulted in a high rate of survival among elderly enslaved folk.

The Voodoo pantheon consists of Bondye, the supreme God, who does not interact with practitioners directly, but does so through a large pantheon of local and patron deities called loa or lwa, deified ancestors, and Catholic saints, who communicate with believers in dreams and trances, as well as possessions during ritual services. During these ritual services a priest or priestess leads adherents, called vodouisants, in ceremonies that can involve song, drumming, dance, prayer, and food preparation. The loa demand these honorific ceremonial services during which they might attach themselves to individuals or families, and the loa, in turn, act as helpers, protectors and guides. The loa are invited to 'mount' or possess worshipers during rituals to dispense advice, perform cures, or display specific physical feats or otherwise make themselves available to the individual or community.

According to Catherine Beyer, an alternative religions expert:

In New World Vodou, the spirits (or lwa) with whom believers interact are divided into three main families: Rada, Petro, and Ghede. Lwa can be viewed as forces of nature, but they also have personalities and personal mythologies. They are extensions of the will of Bondye, the ultimate principle of the universe.

Rada loa have their roots in Africa. These were spirits or deities honored by slaves who were brought to America during the slave trade and these loa became the major spirits in this new religion syncretized in the United States. Rada loa are generally compassionate and creative. They are associated with the color white.

Petro (or Petwo) lwa originate in the New World, specifically in what is now Haiti. As such, they do not appear in African Vodou practices. They are associated with the color red.

Petro lwa tend to be more aggressive and are more often associated with darker subjects and practices.

To divide up the Rada and Petro lwa in terms of good and evil, however, would be highly misrepresenting, and rituals dedicated toward assistance or harm of another can involve lwas of either family.

Ghede loa are associated with the dead and also with carnality. They transport dead souls, behave irreverently, make obscene jokes, and perform dances that mimic sexual intercourse. They teach the celebration of life in the midst of death.

The Ghede are associated with the color black.

The primary goddesses and gods from the Yoruban religion and its dispersion in the Americas are complex and multifaceted. Rhythm and dance are some of many ways used to invite and communicate with these spiritual beings. According to the website Mystic Voodoo:

> In the Voodoo Pantheon, there is an important group of female loa (goddesses) whose first name is Erzulie. While all of them share in their role as goddess of love, art, and sex, each has additional areas of life, which is theirs to defend and assist. Erzulie is three in aspect: She can be Erzulie Freda, a virgin goddess likened to the Virgin Mary; Erzulie Dantor, loa of jealousy and passion; or La Siren, a personification of the sea and goddess of motherhood. Her color is pink. Her animal a white dove. She is associated with the Lukumi (Santeria) Orisha Oshun, and sometimes Chango (as Erzulie Dantor).

In this latter association she is the Petro lwa.

Erzulie Dantor is a mother who watches over and cares for her children with all her heart. She can be a strict disciplinarian as she does not and will not tolerate her children behaving badly. She will defend her children and family to the very end. For very little sacrifice on their part, Dantor will also help a person. She can be a tough lady and a bit wild, but first and foremost she is a mother. She is the most perfect mother one could wish to have.

Dantor is syncretized with the image of Santa Barbara Africana. She is also associated with Madonnas who hold a child such as Our Lady of Mount Carmel and Our Lady of Czestochowa. Other images include Our Lady of Lourdes and Our Lady of Perpetual Help. Dantor is a protector of children and, as naturally as a mother would protect her own, Mama Dantor will always go to extremes to ensure the safety of her children. She will stop everything she is in the process of doing in order to go to her child's aid. Her color correspondences are navy blue and red.

She is featured with a child any time she is depicted, and the daughter most frequently seen in her arms is known as 'Anais'. Anais often serves as Erzulie Dantor's translator and interpreter. She relays messages sent to Dantor, thus she is often directly addressed when wishing to speak to Dantor.

Sometimes people confuse the many Erzulies. Dantor is a spirit that is separate from the others although like most lwa she has many sister spirits that walk with her. There is a long time rivalry between Erzulie Dantor and her sister Erzulie Freda who is syncretized with Our Lady of Sorrows. Like many sisters in real life, there is strong jealousy between them. As the story goes, Dantor and Freda were both courting a particular Ogou Loa. Over this man they fought and never reconciled. In the course of this battle, Dantor took the dagger which she always carries with her and stabbed Freda in the heart. There is evidence of this represented in Freda's saint iconography where a gold dagger is seen coming out from her heart. Freda removed the dagger and cut Dantor's face, scarring her. On the Santa Barbara Africana images you will see scars on her cheek. Although there are only two marks, these marks are often called 'twa mak' or three marks. Facial scarring of this type points to Dantor's African roots where such facial scarring is common.

Granne Erzulie (Grandma Erzulie) represents the wisdom gained by experience and maturity, and grandmotherly kindness and love. She is syncretized with Saint Anne, the mother of the Virgin Mary.

Yemaya is the goddess of the sea and the moon and, like the ocean, when she is angry she can be implacable. Therefore, she represents the mother who gives love, but does not give her own power away. During the Middle Passage, Yemaya was petitioned and thanked for safe arrival in the New World. She is the mother archetype and the provider of abundance. She is generous and charitable as the one who gives life and sustains the Earth. She has a nurturing energy and she is sensuous, calm and soothing much like the ocean. Since she holds the secrets that are hidden in the sea, Yemaya is also the keeper of the collective subconscious and ancient wisdom. She is often invoked in fertility rituals for women and in any ritual concerning women's issues. She is frequently identified with the Catholic Our Lady of the Seafaring and is often worshiped along with her on February 2nd. Her correspondences include that which ebbs and flows: oceans, rivers and other bodies of water, the moon, seashells, fish, and intuitive knowledge. Her numerical correspondence is 7 and her colors are blue, turquoise and white.

Maman Brigitte ('Mother Brigitte') is a Guede goddess who is the wife of Baron Samedi and protector of gravestones or funerary markers. She likes to drink rum infused with hot peppers. Her correspondences include drums and dance, fire, and the color black. She is syncretically associated with Saint Brigit.

Over the centuries, the practice of Voodoo has had to be discreet periodically to a lesser or greater degree due to the misunderstanding of the tenets of this faith path and the subsequent discrimination of its devotees. An example of that is shown here, originally appearing in Harper's Weekly magazine for December 25, 1886, in an article called 'New Orleans Superstitions' by Lafcadio Hearn, which indicates the degree to which Voodoo had become more secretive at that time:

The question 'What is Voudooism?' could scarcely be answered to-day by any resident of New Orleans unfamiliar with the life of the African west coast, or the superstitions of Hayti (Haiti), either through study or personal observation.

The old generation of planters in whose day Voudooism had a recognized existence – so dangerous as a motive power for black insurrection that severe measures were adopted against it – has passed away; and the only person I ever met who had, as a child in his colored nurse's care, the rare experience of witnessing a Voudoo ceremonial, died some three years ago (1883), at the advanced age of seventy-six.

As a religion – an imported faith – Voudooism in Louisiana is really dead; the rites of its serpent worship are forgotten; the meaning of its strange and frenzied chants, whereof some fragments linger as refrains in Negro song, is not now known even to those who remember the words; and the story of its former existence is only revealed to the folklorists by the multitudinous debris of African superstition which it has left behind it. These only I propose to consider now; for what is to-day called Voudooism in New Orleans means, not an African cultus, but a curious class of Negro practices, some possibly derived from it, and others which bear resemblance to the magic of the Middle Ages.

It is of interest to note that Mr. Hearn's article was published five and a half years after the death of Voodoo Queen Marie Laveau who brought Louisiana Voodoo into its 'Golden Age' by turning aspects of her Voodoo practice into a business and popularizing the religion not only among black slaves, but also with the white population as well.

In *New Orleans Voodoo Crossroads* (1994), Reverend Severine Singh states:

> Today about 15% of the population of New Orleans practices Voodoo. Modern Voodoo has taken several directions: Spiritualist Reverends and Mothers who have their own churches, Hoodoos who integrate and work spells and super-stitions, elements of European witchcraft and the occult, and traditionalists for whom the practice of Voodoo is a most natural and important part of their daily lives, a positive search for ancient roots and wisdom. The practice of Voodoo involves the search for higher levels of consciousness in the belief that – as indeed all of the ancient scriptures teach – it is we who must open the way towards the Gods, for when we call out from our hearts, the Gods hear and indeed are compelled to respond. Voodoo is a powerful mystical practice between (Wo)Man and God thus saving her/him from further estrangement from the very universe that s/he is born into.

And more recently from Reverend Severine:

> To this day most Voodooiens are Catholic and continue to blend the spiritual practices that unite the feast days of the Saints with services to the Lwa and/or Orisha, to attend churches and do good works in their communities. This is true in the Caribbean islands as it is in Louisiana, whereas in other parts of the deep South, we see many Voodooists coming out of the Spiritualist churches. There is a reason that our Obatala altars are the highest in our Temple rooms!

Louisiana Voodoo is not simply a spiritual path, but also a religion in the truest sense of the word. It is a way of life that manifests in the day-to-day social, ethical and moral attributes and practices of the adherents of this complex and rich tradition that has its roots in west Africa dating back thousands of years ago and is still evolving today.

Sherrie Almes lives in Alexandria, Virginia and is a Priestess of the Tradition of the Witches Circle in Occoquan, Virginia. She also contributed to *Paganism 101: An Introduction to Paganism by 101 Pagans* and *Naming the Goddess*.

Importing the Goddess: Ariadne in America

One of my earliest spiritual teachers told me, 'Look at where you are and where you've come from. Between them you'll find your truth.' This simple saying has many layers of meaning, but one aspect in particular applies to the topic of this book. Where I am is North America; where I've come from, figuratively speaking, is Europe. From a spiritual perspective, I'm straddling two separate continents. Sometimes that's a pleasant challenge and sometimes it's more of a struggle. I'm pretty sure my teacher didn't mean I would find my truth halfway across the Atlantic Ocean, but it has taken me a lot of time and effort to find that metaphoric middle ground.

I've lived my whole life in the famed American melting pot, one of a huge number of people in this country who have mixed, mostly-European heritage. In fact, several members of my family have put a lot of effort into tracing our ancestry back to its European roots, so I do have a pretty detailed picture of where I'm from in a figurative sense. Also, it's pretty obvious from my appearance where my ancestors came from. My skin is so light, on occasion people have asked me if I'm wearing white stockings (when my legs were actually bare). And I recently had an ancestry DNA test done as well, just to confirm the family tree. So there's no mistaking it. My ancestors were by and large European.

But for many years I never really thought of myself as European in general, much less Irish or British or Scandinavian, even though those are the main regions my ancestors came from. Sure, I'm white. I grew up and still live in the American South, where my heritage and skin color can be a pointed issue at times, thanks to our unfortunate history and the continued difficulties people of color face here in spite of the forward strides the civil rights movement has made. But for many years, whenever I was cornered into putting a label on myself, all I could really come up with was 'American.' I had no particular ethnic identity in spite of knowing where my forebears came from. Like many of the people I knew, I simply saw myself as an average, middle class individual.

In addition to the general lack of ethnic identity, I grew up without a particularly strong religious identity. As a child in 1960s and 70s suburban America, I was immersed in a largely secular society. Christmas was a time for TV specials and presents, not church services. Easter centered around the egg hunt and the freshly-hatched baby chicks on our family farm, not the resurrection of Jesus Christ. Except for a brief time in elementary school when my mother dragged my sister and me to church for a series of Sundays, we had no religious practice to speak of. My family didn't even identify strongly with any specific religion, even though every branch we could trace had been at least nominally Christian, in one form or another, for several centuries. Over the generations the herb women in my family, the ones who quietly kept bits and pieces of folk magic alive, showed up in the pews every now and then to keep up appearances. And members of my grandparents' and great-grandparents' generations devoted themselves to various forms of Christianity including the Methodist and Primitive Baptist traditions. But my age group was largely religion-less.

So, no particular ethnic identity, no particular religious identity. I was a generic American. Simple, right? Then as I grew older I began looking more closely at what that meant, in spiritual terms, and it turned out to be way more complicated than I had expected. I guess that's what I get for thinking too much! So what could possibly be that difficult in terms of a white woman in the United States choosing a spiritual path? After all, freedom has long been a byword in this country. Our famed pioneering spirit of individualism practically requires that Americans do their own thing, whatever that might be, and no one seems to mind very much when that involves combining bits and pieces from a wide variety of sources. My problem was deceptively simple: figure out what 'my own thing' was, in terms of my spiritual path. You might say it was an issue of too many choices. The more closely I examined the situation, the more overwhelmed I felt.

First of all, I live in North America, but I'm not of native North American heritage. The vast majority of my ancestors came here from northwestern Europe in the mid to late 18th century, part of the huge wave of immigrants who descended on these shores and eventually took over the place, for better or for worse. I'm sure my ancestors, like most of their contemporaries, considered this continent to be simply a handy resource put at their disposal to use however they saw fit, a gift from God or the government or both. I doubt they viewed their new home as a living thing with a spirit and vitality that deserves respect and reverence. But I'm Pagan so I feel I must honor the Earth where I live, the wights and land spirits and those whose bones have become a part of this soil over the centuries and millennia. So over the years I've developed a quiet, contemplative practice of daily offerings to the Spirit of the Place. I give my attention and reverence to the Earth itself and to the spirits of life and death that weave through this region, the southeastern United States. Through this practice I've developed a relationship with the land here, even though on the grand scale of history (and prehistory) I'm a relative newcomer.

Unfortunately, this practice alone has never been enough to fill me up spiritually. In addition to respecting the place where I live, I also feel the need to pay reverence to my own ancestors and include them in my spiritual path somehow. They are literally in my blood and in my bones, the DNA I carry in every cell in my body. They are the ones on whose shoulders I stand. But, except for the most recent generations, they're not from North America. For eons their blood and bones have mingled with the soil of a different continent, a place I have only visited briefly. So as I searched for spiritual fulfillment, I was faced with the need to connect with a faraway place, its spirits and powers and deities. This is the 'where I've come from' part of my teacher's comments. Early in my explorations of Paganism, this concept led me to delve into the pantheons from the diverse cultures that fill the history of Europe.

Out of all the culturally-based spiritual paths available to the modern Pagan, information about the Celtic and Norse traditions is fairly easy to come by. Books and websites abound and most Pagans are at least familiar with the basics of these two pantheons, even if they don't practice those traditions themselves. So when I began my explorations of spiritual paths, Celtic and Norse Paganism figured prominently. The groups I belonged to often gravitated towards those pantheons for ritual, whether it was Wiccan-style circles, Norse-style blots or other, less formal occasions. Sure, we occasionally dipped into other cultures – a bit of Mesopotamian here, some Egyptian there – but by and large we stuck to the northwestern European traditions. They were, after all, the paths our ancestors trod.

I have to admit, I enjoyed those rituals. I felt a connection with those deities. As I continued with those practices I sensed I was moving in the right direction, but as time went on I found myself more and more frequently looking over my shoulder, figuratively speaking, feeling like I was missing something that was close by, but that I couldn't quite focus on. You may have experienced this feeling: you keep seeing something out of the corner of your eye, but when you turn your head to look, there's nothing there. Only I was sure there *was* something there. I just wasn't sure exactly what it was. And none of the books and conversations and rituals were helping me figure it out.

We've all had epiphanies, those moments when something finally makes sense so suddenly and clearly that we feel like smacking ourselves in the forehead for not realizing it sooner. Mine came the day I received the assignment for my second degree project in the coven I belonged to at the time. I was required to choose a pantheon – any pantheon – and create a huge collection of rituals using those deities and that culture as the focus. And I do mean huge: a year's worth of seasonal ceremonies and a lifetime's worth of rites of passage.

As I sat there, trying to process the vastness of the work I was being asked to do, I did my best to sift through the various deities and cultures I had encountered so I could choose the pantheon for the assignment. I felt like I was flipping through a card catalog in my mind (yes, I'm that old!) as I mentally tabulated every tradition, every goddess and god I had called to in ritual over the years. So I generated the list in my mind: Celtic, Norse, Anglo-Saxon, Mesopotamian, Egyptian, Hellenic Greek, Roman, even bits of Hindu, Slavic and African. I could practically see all the deities standing around me, like a huge sacred gathering, but I also sensed another presence as well: Minoan. I had never done a ritual with Minoan deities, had never even heard of anyone performing such a ceremony, but in my mind I saw the crowd of gods and goddesses parting, opening a pathway to a scene that took my breath away: the famous Knossos throne room, with Ariadne seated on that throne and Dionysos standing by her side.

I had been fascinated by the ancient Minoans since high school, when my art history teacher introduced me to the vibrant, naturalistic images of the frescoes from Knossos. But I had found very little information about them over the years. The internet was not yet the force it is now and only academics had access to the archaeological journals where the researchers published their findings. There was no modern Minoan Pagan tradition as far as I knew, but I couldn't ignore the call. Almost the moment I made the decision to dedicate my second degree to Ariadne and her tribe, I felt the world shift around me. I knew I had made the right choice. But I still had no idea how to complete the assignment!

My timing was fortuitous (the hand of the gods at work,

perhaps). The archaeologist Nanno Marinatos published her book *Minoan Religion: Ritual, Image and Symbol* later that same year and, when I bought my copy, I felt like I had obtained a great treasure. It's still considered one of the classic references about Minoan religious practices and it gave me the basic information I needed to start putting together the rituals for my assignment. It took the better part of a year, but I managed to create all the required ceremonies and qualify for second degree initiation. What I didn't realize at the time was that was only the beginning of the work.

Over the next decade I performed most of those rituals in various contexts, with friends and members of the Pagan groups I belonged to. And I quickly realized I was going to have to tweak them all pretty carefully in order to make them work well and have the deities be pleased with them. Unlike the more well-known pantheons most of my friends worked with, the Minoan goddesses and gods were enigmatic. We knew so little about them, except the few bits the later Greeks had chewed up and spit out. I was sailing into uncharted territory.

As I took one step and then another into down the path of Minoan Paganism, I discovered several issues with transporting a set of deities across space and time from their original culture. I'm sure the Pagans who did the early work with other pantheons in the modern world experienced similar challenges, but it was a brand new experiment for me. In dealing with these challenges, I learned a great deal about the gods and goddesses of ancient Crete.

The first thing I discovered is that deities are used to being carried around the world as people and cultures shift and move. Think about it: Cybele journeyed from her native Phrygia to Greece and its many colonies. Isis voyaged as far away from Egypt as London. Mithras traveled from his native Persia across the entire Roman Empire. The Minoans got around as well, carrying their trade goods and religious practices around the

Mediterranean and farther afield. Even in ancient times, Ariadne and her tribe had already become world travelers.

So I learned that the goddesses and gods of ancient Crete didn't mind being carried from their native land to my home in North America. But I also learned that importing deities is very much like importing tropical plants: if the climates clash, things can get messy.

If I buy a potted plant, say a croton (Codiaeum variegatum pictum) that's native to the rainforests of the Pacific islands and Malaysia, I have to recognize that it needs a warm and humid environment or it will die. Now, the gods won't die if I don't water them properly (thank heavens), but they do come from specific environments that can clash with the seasons in other parts of the world. The island of Crete lies in the eastern Mediterranean and experiences a climate unlike that of my native North America. That turned out to be a sticking point.

Eastern North America, where my ancestors settled and where my family still lives, is part of the northern temperate zone. We experience the well-known seasonal cycle of spring, summer, autumn and winter, with warm summers and mild winters compared, say, to the US Upper Midwest. My ancestors in the British Isles would have been familiar with these seasons. But the ancient Minoans would have found them quite foreign.

The Mediterranean climate is closer in nature to tropical than temperate environments. The year is loosely divided into wet and dry seasons, with the rains beginning in the late autumn and finishing up in the spring. Summers are hot and dry; the plants turn crispy-brown and creeks dry up. In the Mediterranean the summer, not the winter, is the dead season. On Crete, farmers sow their crops in the autumn. The plants grow with the help of the winter rains and are harvested in the spring. That's quite a contrast to the agricultural cycle where I live. In fact, the only part of the US that experiences a Mediterranean climate is the southernmost part of California. I've never even visited there.

One of the mainstays of Paganism in general involves honoring the Earth. In order to honor the land where I live, I celebrate the seasonal cycles of North America. But I also acknowledge the wheel of the year in Crete, even if I don't live it. So when I organize a Spring Equinox ritual with a Minoan focus, I make sure to share with the participants that the people of Crete would have held that kind of celebration in the autumn. My friends and I celebrate the harvest in the autumn, but I always recall that the Minoans brought in their crops during the other half of the year. In some ways, I feel like I'm dealing with a situation similar to Pagans in Australia who follow the eightfold European wheel of the year, but reverse the dates to fit the sabbats to their local environment.

One issue that continues to strike me as vital in Paganism in general, but Minoan spirituality in particular, is gender equality. The Goddess was pushed into the shadows for so long, but thankfully even the concerted efforts of powerful institutions couldn't destroy her. In recent times Earth-oriented spirituality has brought her back into the light, reminding us of the paradigm in which feminine and masculine are equally sacred and equally valuable. The Minoans especially provide a powerful image of a peaceful, egalitarian society, a kind of culture we can aspire to and work towards. In my lifetime I've seen women break many societal bonds, but we still have a long way to go toward true equality. I'd like to think Ariadne and her tribe have our backs as we march forward. If we honestly want this to be the land of the free and the home of the brave, we need the gods to walk with us along the way.

Through more than two decades of working with the Minoan deities and sharing my life with them, I've come to realize that they understand more than we might think. They recognize the passage of time, the fact that the world changes over the ages as individuals and cultures shift, grow, move and die. They know the society I live in has values and conventions that contrast with ancient Crete, sometimes strongly, sometimes just in the details. But they also understand that deep within each of us lies a spirit, a sense of humanity that we share in common with every other person, living or dead. Though I may be removed from the ancient Minoans by thousands of miles and thousands of years, I still have the same kinds of hopes and dreams they did. I still long for meaning and purpose, love and companionship, kindness and compassion. Like the gods, these things stand the test of time and happily settle wherever we choose to take them.

Laura Perry is a Wiccan priestess, and long-time pagan and shamanic practitioner. She is also a Reiki master, herbalist, and naturopath (N.D.) and author of *Ariadne's Thread*.

The Hebrew Goddess in America

If you ask me, yes, of course there are Old World goddesses in America.

Whether or not they accompanied people who came to America is an open question, one I am not here to answer. But I will say this. People who follow alternative spirituality, even priestesses who I may naively expect to know better, believe that all the goddesses are one. Some believe that one goddess manifests in all the thousands of ways in which people through the ages have seen goddesses. This may be a nice thought, but this belief is one which my tradition, AMHA, does not share. We consider this a form of monotheism.

The view of goddesses as one has opened the door to unintentional cultural misappropriation. That is, well-intentioned people have borrowed from someone else's tradition without a true knowledge and understanding of what that tradition says. Although this is rarely intended to be disrespectful, to the inheritor of the tradition it may sometimes feel that way. It does, sometimes, to me.

Goddesses show many faces to humans, as do gods. When someone says to me that a given goddess from our Traditional Pantheon is exactly the same (as opposed to sharing some similarities) as a Divinity from another Pantheon, I balk. People are not the same, nor are gods. Otherwise, what a boring world ours would be...

I would like to introduce you to some of the goddesses from my Tradition. Their roots are in my birthplace, the Levant, located in today's western Middle East, in Israel and its surroundings. This is where they originated.

They have traveled to America with us and many others.

My Goddesses, still relatively unknown here, are Hebrew Goddesses. Yes, please understand what I am saying. There are

Hebrew Goddesses, and Canaanite (our first cousins), too, right here in America.

Is this so hard to believe...Hebrew Goddesses?

Yes, indeed. Contrary to the opinion of biblical authors and subsequent clergy of various religions, etc, the ancient Hebrews where not monotheists like modern Christians, Muslims, or rabbinical Jews. They were, in the words of a mainstream secular scholar, 'polytheists.'

AMHA, or Primitive Hebrews, is a Hebrew earth tradition reconnected to the tribes from the time before monotheism began. Indeed, we had a Goddess. In fact, we had and still have, in our modern version of that tradition, more than one.

One is Ashera, also known as Asherah or Asherat. The other is Rahmay. There are more, but I will limit this article to these two Ladies of Power.

Ashera

I will tell you about the Lady Ashera first. Rank has its privileges...

First and foremost, Lady Ashera's titles have included 'Queen of Heaven,' 'She who walks upon the waters,' and, significantly, 'Mother of all the Gods.' In modern terms, Ashera is the boss Lady, ruling over gods and humans alike.

We have rituals to honor Her. One day a week is Her day. We honor many Powers of our ancient Tradition, especially our Ancestors. Regardless of personal devotion, She has precedence on our little personal altars, on which we have images of either Ashera or Her symbols. As Mother of the Gods, She also has precedence in our rituals.

We greet Her in the morning and before retiring in the evenings. We burn incense to Her (daily, if we can) and sometimes offer her libations when blessing or having ritual meals. We thank Her for Her abundance after meals.

Ashera was the wife of the Great God El, himself an old, lusty, kind, compassionate Father God. El was known as the 'Ancient of Days,' meaning Ancient One, which was a title of honor in the early Middle East. He was also the kind God, the 'God who is filled with Mercy' (meaning compassion). Those who believe El to be vengeful, destructive, and given to directing His people to genocidal acts are quite mistaken. That image of El was invented later, and is a topic for another article.

Like Fathers, even good ones, in the traditional world and today, El is relatively absent from day-to-day matters. Although He is kind, He is a mighty God. That, of course, intimidates people. Out of respect, one does not take smaller complaints to the El Elohim, the God of Gods.

Understandably, in fear of asking El directly, humans and gods alike went to the Lady Ashera for help, not because he was not kind. Rather, this was because as his wife, and as Mother Goddess, She had influence over him greater than that of humans or other gods. As a result, one tends to assume that it is appropriate to go to the Great Mother of Gods, although she rules as Goddess of All.

In one of our stories, when young Baal (a title, not a name, of a weather and storm God who was indistinguishable from Yahwe in his earliest forms) wants a palace like all the other Gods, he goes to Mother Ashera to complain that El has not allowed him one. She puts on her loveliest clothes and strides off to have dinner with El. She persuades him to allow that palace to be built.

You have probably understood by this point that 'Mother' in those days was not the romantic, delicate little figure of Victorian imagination, lovingly cradling a little baby and needing some big strong Dad to protect them both. This Mother is, in strong contrast, a Lady of Power. We revered her as such back home in Israel. We revere Her as such here in the States, as well. I have seen her depicted on some pagan pages as some sort of sex kitten. Panther, perhaps. Kitten, no.

For the Canaanites, first cousins to the Hebrews, who had a

high civilization with temples and a priesthood and all the trimmings of a rich culture, Ashera was Queen of Heaven.

For the Hebrews, who were poorer, tribal, less advanced culturally, and had neither kings nor queens, she would more likely have been the female Chieftain of their tribes, full counterpart to the male Chieftain God. This is the aspect we AMHA, as Primitive Hebrews, are drawn to.

Ashera also has a warrior aspect. On some incense burners found in Israel She is, for example, depicted as a naked Goddess flanked by two lions. The lion was one of Her companion animals.

In the ancient western Middle East that I refer to, a companion animal always reveals something about the character of their companion God or Goddess. Indeed, who hunts for the cubs? Who fiercely defends them? The female lion. An interesting note is that 'lion,' at one point in Hebrew history, was a term denoting warriors, and this seems further evidence of Ashera's warrior aspect.

There is a bust of Ashera, found in Tel Erani, Israel, that shows her in an Egyptian wig, which is a short practical wig that reaches to just below the ears. Over the wig She is wearing a helmet, as a warrior would have worn in the Egyptian-dictated fashion of the time. The short Egyptian wig would have made excellent padding upon which to set a war helmet. It would help absorb blows, and also prevent the Middle Eastern sun from cooking you through the heated metal. As Raphael Patai pointed out in his famous book *The Hebrew Goddess*, 'The Hebrew Goddess lies in the fact that the Shekhina of modern rabbinical Jews, the female face of God, has an aspect of warrior and severity, as the Talmud says.'

Since there is no war being waged on United States land, we do not attend to Ashera's warrior aspect as much here. Another Goddess, Anat, is associated more with war, but she is not our topic. Regardless of which aspect speaks to you, the Lady Ashera is a mighty one.

How do we know that Ashera was revered by the Hebrews, and later the Jews? First of all, literature tells us. She is mentioned more than thirty times in the Hebrew Bible. In the King James translation her name is often replaced with the term 'groves.' Groves were sacred to Her. I will discuss Her connection with trees later. Our next source is archeology. We know that in the houses of the Hebrews, there were small statues of Ashera for intimate, personal worship. Over a thousand of these 'pillar figurines' of Ashera were discovered in archeological digs in the past forty or so years. Some were found earlier, but at that time archeologists did not yet understand that this was Ashera. Also, the majority (seven hundred or so) of these statuettes intended for private worship, were found in the area of Jerusalem, supposedly a bastion of monotheism.

How do we know this was not a 'foreign Goddess,' as She is referred to in some sections of the Hebrew Bible? Ashera was found associated with incense altars in the houses of those who lived next door to the great Jerusalem Temple. You would not expect a commoner to live there. Indeed, this is what the archeologists found. She was found in the houses of nobles and of priests of high rank, people important and influential enough that they built their homes beside the Temple in Jerusalem, a most desirable address. So much for monotheism...

An important aspect of Ashera, one which the Victorians just loved to be shocked about, is seen in the 'pillar figurines' I have mentioned. These statuettes are often only a handspan high, and only a bust (i.e., a head, shoulders, arms, and chest), with the invariable short wig or hair style, a serene smile on her face, stylized arms holding up her breast. The rest of Her body is simply a cylinder...hence, 'pillar figurines.'

Oh, the Victorians must have drooled. They called these, 'fertility' statues.

Hmmmm...yes and no. When they said, 'fertility,' they really meant a sex Goddess. After all, her breasts were bare. They did not, of course, use that impolite term. They put skirts on piano legs, after all.

But Ashera was not a sex Goddess. She may have had an aspect of this. There may also have been another Goddess, known as Qedesh or Qedesha, which means Holy One. She represents the aspect of sexual energy, but not only that. This, too, is another story. Sex being sacred in our Tradition, we revere Her, too.

So what is suggested by those offered breasts? Ashera herself, remember, is a mother. And this is precisely how She is depicted. If you look closely at those breasts that she is holding up, they are not the young perky breasts of a young woman who has never yet conceived nor breast-fed. They are, rather, the heavy breasts of someone who has been a mother, who has breast-fed, and whose breast are no longer maidenly and perky.

Ashera is not a young female Goddess, like the war Goddess, Anat. She is a full-grown woman, and the All Mother. She nourishes All. She is holding up her breast not to titillate, but to show that with her milk, she is sustaining both Gods and humans.

In creating the pillar statuettes, branches were cut from a tree, leaving the trunk. The bust, head, and arms of the Goddess were set on top of the trunk. She was presumably decorated with jewelry and, perhaps, fine clothing. In the south of Israel, where there would have been far fewer trees than in the fertile north, they would simply have made a terracotta tree trunk and set her bust on it. Hence, pillar figurines.

Ashera is also powerfully associated with trees. Groves of trees were planted in Her honor. Trees were also planted in locations of worship. The admonition, 'Thou shall not plant an Ashera next to the altar,' proves that people did.

In the art of Israel, scholars in that part of the world agree that a downward-pointing triangle represents female divinity. It is often flanked by ibexes, wild goats with beautiful curved horns.

The ibexes represent wild nature, and they feed from the triangle. This design is often alternated with a five- or seven-branched tree, also flanked by ibexes. It is understood by scholars that when figures alternate in this way, they mean the same thing. So, the triangular goddess symbol is very closely associated with trees.

Her name, 'Ashera' means something like abundance or opulence, and is also related to happiness. Indeed, there appears to have been a special association with the abundance of fruit trees, especially figs, pomegranates and date palms, all of which either give much fruit or have many seeds. In my Tradition we sing to Ashera and plant seedlings or trees on the New Year of the Trees, known as Tu Be Shevat.

The memory of all of this is in the Menorah, the seven-branched candelabrum that was in the Jewish Temple. The menorah is still the symbol of the State of Israel, and stands in front of the parliament.

The Menorah, which, according to the Hebrew Bible, was made in the semblance 'of a flowering tree' has preserved the memory of our Hebrew Goddess to this day.

Rahmay

It is difficult to complain about modern cultural misappropriation when it comes to the next Goddess I want to tell you about, whose name is Rahmay She is so little known in the West that She has escaped, so to speak, numerous attempts to turn Goddesses into cartoon or comic book images of their ancient selves.

The Goddess Rahmay, too, comes from our homeland, the area that is today Syria, Israel, Jordan, and Lebanon, or the western Levant, the east coast of the Mediterranean Sea.

According to some important German scholars in their book, *Gods, Goddesses, and Images of God in Ancient Israel*, Rahmay is a very ancient Goddess. In fact, She is so ancient that she is, at once, the Earth-as-Goddess *and* the Goddess of Earth. Later in history these concepts became separate ones.

Three images of her have been found in Israel. They are intact enough that you can see immediately why she is named Rahmay. 'Rahmay' means 'womb.' Indeed, She is shown naked, as Goddesses were shown in the ancient Mid East, with her hands holding her womb open, to signify that she is one who constantly brings forth life.

There are two adult humans hanging from her breasts to show She sustains the human life She birthed. On each of Her thighs is a palm tree, flanked by Ibexes who are feeding from that palm, meaning that She is the Mother of plant life that feeds not only humanity, but also the animal world as well.

Rahmay, the Womb of All Life, the Mother of Life, and of Life Force in its many, many forms…just think about Her.

Think of the power of Life Force. A dead tree falls, and is immediately colonized, first by microbes, which reproduce, and then by fungi, which also reproduce. All sorts of little creatures feed those, who in turn reproduce and feed others. The tree has barely fallen when the Power of Life surges. The recycling of what was once alive causes more and more rich life to flourish. Death supporting life is a constant process, one that is going on everywhere around us, every second, every minute of every day. The awesome power of generating life is active in millions of ways everywhere on the globe, including within your own body as you drew one breath while reading this. It is unstoppable, and there is no other Force like it.

On and on that great Life Energy pulsates and grows things, even in the depth of the sea, even in temperatures so hot we once thought nothing could live there, and in places so cold we thought life could not exist there. In our Tradition, it is all Rahmay's power, Rahmay's energy creating and animating all.

To me, she is the most awe-inspiring Force I can think of. How can one think of Her, of what She is, and not feel awe?

We revere her. We sing to her before the Ritual of Seeing for the Tribes. We sing to her before starting any ritual at all. I have carved her form onto a wooden stela, faithfully copying what our Ancestors attempted to represent when they sculpted Her. She has an altar all Her own in my meditation space, and some fragments of lava and some small fossils are beside her sculpture, further symbolizing the eternity and All Power of She who births Life.

In Hebrew we chant (continental transliteration):

Ela Rahmay
Ela Rahmay
Em col Hai

Goddess Rahmay
Goddess Rahmay
Mother of Life

Elisheva Nesher is the current Shophet of AMHA (Primitive Hebrew Assembly) USA.

Part 3

The Relational Goddess

The Goddess and the Feminist

In her seminal essay 'Why Women Need the Goddess,' thealogian Carol P. Christ famously intoned, 'Because religion has such a compelling hold on the psyches of many people, feminists cannot afford to leave it in the hands of the fathers. Even people who no longer 'believe in God' or participate in the institutional structure of patriarchal religion may still not be free from the symbolism of God the Father.' The power of the symbol of God the Father, Christ argued, exerts powerful influence over the minds and hearts of people in cultures that revere him, even if they do not worship him themselves. The only way to break the hold of the symbol of God the Father, and by extension the patriarchal values that he represents, was to find power in new symbols. For many Americans, particularly American women, that new powerful symbol is the Goddess. Whether they find Her in Wicca, in Feminist Separatist Witchcraft, or in informal living room circles where the Divine Feminine is celebrated in a myriad personal ways, Americans have found in Goddess-centered spirituality a way to go, as thealogian Mary Daly famously put it, 'beyond God the Father.'

The question of whether or not a Goddess-centered spirituality is inherently feminist is a fraught one, and one that is roundly and hotly debated in the American Pagan community. Because American Paganism encompasses a wide variety of practices, lifestyles, and political viewpoints, there is no single right answer. Some (this author among them) argue that claiming a Feminine Godhead is inherently a feminist act and that it is inseparable from feminist politics and concerns about real human women (and people of all genders, in fact). Others argue that venerating a Goddess, almost always alongside a God, is key to bringing balance to the Universe, but that gender complementarity is a fact of nature – that men and women have their roles, and that these are reflections of a Divine Order, and that human political movements have little or nothing to do with their understanding of spirituality.

What is key to understand, however, is the key role that feminism – in particular the second wave feminist movement of the 1970s and early 1980s – played in the development of American Paganism as we know it. Whether or not individual Pagans or Pagan traditions consider themselves feminist – and even if they consider themselves anti-feminist! – they owe a great cultural debt to feminists and feminist thought. The roots of the Pagan revival may lie in Gerald Gardner's work in the 1940s and 1950s, but it is the American counterculture, and especially the feminist movement, that gave rise to the uniquely American form of Paganism we see in the United States today. And while not all Goddess-centered spirituality is Pagan, the roots of Goddess spirituality (sometimes called Women's Spirituality or Feminist Spirituality) are intricately and inextricably intertwined with American Paganism, each fostering the growth of the other.

It is impossible to tell, of course, when the first seeds of Goddess-centered spirituality were sown in the Americas. Indigenous people have many traditions around powerful female figures, such as the Lakota White Buffalo Calf Woman or the Navajo Changing Woman. Many American Goddess worshipers consider these traditions part of their lineage. The roots of the American Wiccan movement are generally said to lie with Raymond Buckland, starting in the 1960s, but there are many practitioners who assert family traditions that are much, much older than this, and even American Gardnerian covens that date their founding to well before Buckland arrived in the country. If we are to look for the roots of an explicitly feminist Goddess spirituality, however, we find them in the feminist movement of the 1970s, though they were undoubtedly percolating below the surface well before.

As early as 1974, women in the feminist movement were

expressing interest in the Goddess, some perhaps spurred by Mary Daly's groundbreaking 1973 volume *Beyond God the Father*. The first journal dedicated to what was coming to be termed 'Women's Spirituality,' *WomanSpirit*, began publication in 1974, and the first women's spirituality conference was held in 1975. That same year, Zsuzsanna Budapest, widely credited as the mother of Feminist Witchcraft in America, was arrested for fortune-telling (which was illegal under municipal by-law); she was found guilty. On appeal, the core tenet of her defense lay in establishing Wicca, and particularly Dianic or Feminist Wicca, as a legitimate religion, of which Tarot reading was a key practice, as it represented 'women counseling women.' The guilty verdict was overturned by the California Supreme Court as a violation of the Freedom of Religion Act. Feminism and Goddess worship have arguably been intertwined in the American Pagan imagination and community ever since. Budapest's Dianic Wicca involved covens comprised solely of women, a tradition that continues today (though it is not uncontested in American Pagan circles, especially Dianic Wicca's exclusion of trans women).

The partnership of American Paganism and feminist politics was further cemented with the publication of Starhawk's essay 'Witchcraft and Women's Culture' and book *The Spiral Dance: The Rebirth of the Religion of the Great Goddess*, both in 1979. *The Spiral Dance* has arguably become the foundational text for the American Pagan movement. Infused as it is with Starhawk's only intersectional feminist politics, especially around issues of ecological and gender justice, *The Spiral Dance* brought feminism into mixed-gender Pagan groups. The feminist politics put forth in *The Spiral Dance*, and in the Reclaiming Collective tradition founded by Starhawk, were arguably more appealing to many American Pagans than Budapest's separatist ethos. Reclaiming Collective groups can be composed of members of any gender, for instance, and focus on Goddess veneration (along with a God) as a tool for personal and social change. Many Pagan groups (and individual practitioners) who may not consider their practice to be overtly 'feminist' take *The Spiral Dance* as one of their foundational texts, with the result that at least some feminist ethos is infused in much of American Paganism, especially Wicca and Wicca-based traditions.

Perhaps the key intersection of Goddess-centered spirituality (Pagan and non) and feminist politics lies in the reclamation and celebration of values and characteristics long coded as 'feminine' or 'female' in Western consciousness and particularly in Western religions. Those things relegated to the 'feminine' side of the gender binary – nature, the body and its functions, emotionality, nurturing and caregiving, intuition, and so much more – have also been traditionally relegated to a lower status than those things considered 'masculine.' In the Goddess, women found a celebration of all that Western society and religion had told them they must transcend or suppress in order to be fully human. The Goddess provided a model by which women could feel they had been made in Divine image without having to find ways to act and be more like men. As philosopher Simone de Beauvoir wrote in her classic *The Second Sex*, the image of God the Father legitimates patriarchal power – it 'demonstrates' the naturalness of men's power over women. Through the Goddess, women find not only a way to see the Divine in themselves – what Patricia Lynn Reilly terms 'a God who looks like me' in her book of the same name – but also a model for an alternative power structure. For feminists actively working for social change, to alter or even uproot the existing power structures in society, this symbol has potent spiritual and political power.

Christ asserts that the symbol of the Goddess 'undergirds and legitimates' feminist concerns, largely by allowing a space for women to reclaim and reframe aspects of themselves that have been denigrated by Western culture and theology. Goddess concerns are feminist concerns, in other words, and the Goddess provides a model for addressing these concerns in the world.

Goddess spirituality provides a context in which feminine power is considered legitimate, and does not need to approximate masculine power in order to be respected. Starhawk makes the distinction between 'power over' and 'power with,' characterizing feminine power as 'power with' – power that is derived not from domination but through consensus and community building, power that is drawn from within. While women have gone on to take on clergy and leadership roles in many Western religions traditions since the 1970s, for a time Goddess spirituality groups presented one of the few places where women could assume religious leadership, whether of other groups or even of themselves. Goddess spirituality also relies heavily on women's experiences and personal authority, allowing for a level of religious and spiritual self-determination that many women found (and still find) lacking in the faiths of their past. Even today, American Paganism places great value on personal experience, intuition, and innovation – hallmarks of Feminist Spirituality that are not always found in more traditional Wiccan groups, speaking to its feminist heritage.

The affirmation of the power of women's bodies and women's life cycles, including the experiences of menstruation, childbirth, and menopause, also speaks to the feminist nature of Goddess Spirituality. While the association of these life events and processes solely with women has begun to be contested within American Paganism as notions of gender expand beyond the gender binary, there is little debate that reclaiming the sacredness of bodies that have so often been characterized as inferior or unclean has tremendous healing power. Within Feminist Witchcraft traditions such as Dianic Wicca, the 'mysteries' of bleeding take on central importance, providing a space for women to heal the deep personal and cultural wounds that result from a systematic devaluation and abuse of women and women's bodies. Within Goddess Spirituality, women are able for perhaps the first time to see their own bodies as sacred, as reflections of the body of the Goddess herself. Processes that are laden with shame in the larger culture become subjects of celebration and even veneration, and long-standing silences are broken. (The Red Tent Movement, inspired by Anita Diamant's novel *The Red Tent*, represents just one example of the ways women are using Goddess Spirituality and Goddess symbolism to re-sacralize stigmatized aspects of the female body.)

In re-sacralizing the female body, Goddess Spirituality also speaks to larger feminist concerns of bodily autonomy, reproductive justice, and gender justice, and is explicitly politicized around these issues. Drawing on a long sacred history of women as healers and midwives, Goddess Spirituality encourages women to take back power over their own bodies, their own reproduction, and their own sexuality. Whether by encouraging the exploration of herbal healing, particularly for reproductive health, as in the work of Susun Weed, or conducting private ritual to heal individual women from the traumas of rape and sexual violation, or engaging in public ritual and spellcasting to end a series of rapes in a public park (as in the famous example from Z. Budapest's coven), practitioners of Goddess Spirituality engage in a religiosity that is fundamentally and overtly political and organized around feminist concerns. Environmental issues are also often front and center, particularly with Reclaiming Collective groups, as Goddess Spirituality is heavily informed by ecofeminist thought. The explicit equation of the Earth Herself with the bodies of human women – that the Earth is, as Dianic Priestess Ruth Barrett says, 'a dancing woman' – links the treatment and fate of the Earth with the treatment and fate of women. Indeed, many of the sacred histories upon which Goddess Spirituality draws find the root of our current social ills in the systematic domination of the Earth, and of human women, by patriarchy. While it is hotly contested as to whether these sacred histories, which posit the existence of peaceful, Goddess worshipping matriarchies, are based in historical fact, these narratives provide powerful underpinning for an Earth-centered, Goddess-centered spirituality and alternative model for society. Environmental and feminist politics also intersect in activism, pointing out that women (and children) suffer the worst consequences of globalization and 'development' by far, and that the environmental degradation that results from these processes is part and parcel of the degradation of the world's most vulnerable. Examples of activism include actions taken by Starhawk and other Reclaiming Collective members at the meetings of the World Trade Organization and the G8 Summit.

The feminist maxim that 'the personal is political' is at the heart of much Goddess Spirituality and Feminist Witchcraft, whether it be examining the ways in which personal experiences of sexism and violence are reflective or larger systems of abuse, or in the connections women find between their individual stories and the larger narrative of what is happening to the Earth and the other creatures that live upon her. The symbol of the Goddess, and Goddess rituals, provide a context for these personal experiences. They also provide tools for social change, whether on a larger scale by disrupting globalization or environmental destruction, or on a more personal level by allowing women to re-envision their relationships and ties to one another. Christ points out that one of the major tenets of Goddess Spirituality is the value it places on the bonds between women and the ways it encourages women to form and nurture loving bonds rather than subscribing to the larger Western cultural narrative of women as competition for one another. By creating places where women can be with other women, from small living room circles to large festivals, Goddess Spirituality encourages women to come together, to tell their stories, and to see one another as allies. This spirit of co-operation is echoed in the organization of many Goddess Spirituality and other Pagan groups, with rotating leadership, consensus decision-making, and shared power.

The feminist history of Goddess Spirituality in America is not uncomplicated. As the second wave of American feminism gave way to the third wave, many of the foundational texts and teachers came under scrutiny for their reliance on biological essentialism and the gender binary, and for the lack of intersectionality in their work, which critics (sometimes rightly) say erases the importance of race, class, dis/ability, sexual orientation, and other salient statuses in favor of a mythical universal 'women's experience.' The place of trans women in Feminist Spirituality has also been hotly contested, with some key founders of Goddess Spirituality stating that trans women are not welcome in their rituals and even that they have no place practicing 'women's spirituality.' Issues of cultural appropriation have also been a topic for discussion, as some early writers borrowed freely and not always accurately from indigenous American and African traditions. At the beginning of the 21st century, these issues are still being argued and resolved, against the backdrop of a larger cultural backlash against feminism in many ways. How the next generation of American Pagans, and particularly those who engage in Goddess Spirituality or Feminist Spirituality, will negotiate them remains to be seen.

It is key, however, that this heritage not be forgotten or dismissed. Every intellectual movement is a product of its time, and Goddess Spirituality as it has been known is certainly largely a product of the mid-20th century. But it also has the capacity to evolve and change, as religious movements do, because it is largely shaped by the experiences and will of the individual practitioners. Placing spiritual authority in the hands of individual women rather than in a hierarchy or sacred text allows for tremendous flexibility and innovation. It gives us permission to, in the words of Monique Wittig in Les Guerilleres, 'Make an effort to remember. Or, failing that, invent.'

Susan Harper, Ph.D is an educator, activist, advocate, and ritual facilitator living in the Dallas, Texas area. She holds a doctorate in anthropology and teaches courses in anthropology, sociology, and women's studies, as well as facilitating rituals in the Feminist Spirituality and Feminist Witchcraft tradition. She serves as the Graduate Reader/Editor for Texas Woman's University.

The Goddess and the Shaman

Spider Woman has always been my spiritual grandmother though I learned her name in the latter half of my life. She names me, mentors me and protects me. I know I am not her only granddaughter, far from it, but I am one. Oddly I am a white woman and she is an American Goddess of the Hopi, Navajo, and Keresan people. I understand those who guard her stories and claim her as their own may resent my intrusion. In my defense, she came to me. She was there before I knew such things were possible.

Our conscious relationship began when I was planting annuals in my flower garden soon after starting on the pagan path. At the same time I was wondering about a magical name. My priestess called herself Athena, but refused to name any of us.

'The Goddess will name you when you are ready,' she said.

Certain I was ready, I called out to the great Lady as I planted artemesia and impatiens atop the windflower rhizomes, little brown nutlike things that are hard as stone and take weeks to germinate if they are planted in the spring. The flowering plants were meant to satisfy my lust for beauty while I awaited the windflowers.

'What is my name, Goddess?' I asked realizing I was as impatient as my flowers. Because I didn't know her name either I doubted she would answer. Ignorant lout that I was, I stuck the trowel into the dirt and started another round of pretty pink blooms. The windflowers would poke up among them in shades of peach and blue.

'Webweaver,' she said out of nowhere. 'You may be called Webweaver because you will pull the strands of being together for yourself and others. You have also a secret name. It is there in front of you.'

I picked up the package from the windflowers and saw their

real name: Anemone.

'Don't tell anyone until you understand it. Then wait until I allow it. You'll see why later. Be content with Webweaver.'

I was so astonished I forgot to ask her who she was.

Back in ritual circle I told people my new public name and never mentioned there was another. I admit to being pleased with the title of Webweaver. I had already put out a short monthly mailing called *Webnotes* so members of Athena's circle would know the schedule and the news. We thought of our workings as explorations in consciousness along the witches' path, though some were decidedly more interested in Native American practices. Athena was both, a hereditary Irish witch and a descendant of the Cherokee. We learned rituals her grandmother taught her and magic her parents practiced at migrant camp bonfires. Eventually I discovered it was my great grandmother who also taught me, but not only my human mother's mother's mother. It was the Grandmother Spider, the weaver of the universal web, and I was her apprentice weaver.

In addition to naming me, Spider Woman mentors my education. She sent me researching my flowers in a quest to understand my secret name Anemone. Not only were anemones beautiful, tenacious windflowers, there were sea anemones that held a special metaphor to describe my spiritual life's work. Sea anemones come in lush colors and in a wide variety of shapes. They look like underwater flowers though they are animals of the order *Actiniaria*. Along with this diversity, they reproduce both sexually and asexually in a variety of ways. Most of those have a message for me, because the task Spider Woman set before me is to teach others and spin them off on their own to weave the web in a similar way. Sea anemones reproduce by dividing in two to create an equal twin. Alternatively they break off a piece of themselves which will grow small clones. Sometimes a sea anemone shares its own eggs and sperm to create a new individual with the same DNA. Once I studied this out as spiritual metaphor, my employer assigned me a computer user name: dna. Not my initials, but a cosmic joke I came to appreciate, one that confirmed I wasn't making this all up.

The long and short of it was Spider Woman expected me to share my discoveries, her teachings really, with other people who would take them to heart and make webs with them. Egotistically I thought we would all remain connected in a loving organization that spanned the country. I forgot how independent minded pagans are. It is she who is the Grandmother Spider, not me. Some people have stayed to weave this web with me. Others travelled back home or relocated to Florida. A few decided never to speak to me again and more gave me excessive credit for everything they do. Instead of making a human organization centered at my Web, the group cloned itself and spread out on the currents of consciousness to start over their own way. It is all the same. All have taken lessons to heart and created pagan circles seasoned with their own life experience where they can draw friends and students together and weave their connections to spirit.

Reportedly one of them groused, 'How do we get out of the Web?' I laughed. One can leave our place and our circle, but one can never leave the over soul web of consciousness. That is the fabric all of us weave as a tapestry telling life's epiphanies. Through these we wake up to find we are all still connected with a sort of spiritual DNA that transcends anything one little circle sews together. It is a larger weaving that spirals us into the center of being and jars our souls alert to the endless possibilities of magic. That transformation is the working of the Grandmother.

So I was named Webweaver and Anemone and given a life mission by Grandmother Spider. I journeyed with her and learned more science about sea anemones and spiders, which reminded me of how to do the things she set before me. First among those lessons was to stop being squeamish about spiders in the house. We negotiated places they could live and catch insects in peace. Sometimes my cats ate them anyway. Spiders that spread outside of their secure area were sucked up by the vacuum. I have lost count of how many spiders spontaneously appeared in ritual circle to join the festivities. They challenge people who are not yet connected to the natural world. Such occasions become opportunities to teach about 'ALL my relations.'

In addition to naming me and then teaching me, Grandmother Spider protects me. That too is a teaching. In 2004 I fell dangerously ill with respiratory failure and ended up hospitalized. All the wonders of modern science could not name what was wrong with me, though they treated the symptoms and got me back on my feet. In the process I received some surprising lessons from two male spirits she sent to carry the messages. How I heard her truths and opened them up so I could understand them takes more telling than I can offer here, but I will share the insights.

First, there are entities sent to challenge us when we are vulnerable. People call them by many negative names. I encountered one in hospital. I called him a soul stealer and I was afraid. He attached himself to a hospital staff person working nights as a phlebotomist. I didn't believe in such things until I saw him laughing in the doorway. When these spirits arrive, our guards and guides arrive right on their tails. A circle of spirit wolves tracked around my bed and one of my Native American guides stood 10 feet tall behind me. My soul stayed safely in place and I slept because I could do nothing else. Soul stealer left and never came back. Maybe he worked a different wing or another shift, but I never saw him again.

Second, we offer service to our allies in important ways. One of my guides lost a friend in death while I was in the hospital. He saw her to the entrance and watched her cross over to the next life, but could not leave earth himself. I approached him at the door of the hospital in a dream and comforted him. He stepped into me and let me carry him for weeks while he healed. When I left the hospital myself, I saw the front entrance for the first time. It was what I'd seen in the dream. I knew exactly where he'd stood, where his friend had walked, how I had approached. He stirred in my heart as if to say, 'Yes.' I had not made it up. It was no fantasy.

Third, there is a mystery between windflowers, breath, creative work and the Gods. As I was recording the lessons learned in the hospital in my Book of Shadows, I was challenged to understand yet another name. This was Grandmother speaking in my ear again. She had released me to use the name Anemone and to hand over the shuttle of web-weaving to someone else so I could recover and write about her webs. We performed ceremony to that end. Then I set out to understand what name encompassed my favorite flowers, my writing, my respiratory challenges and my Gods. It took a while.

Eventually I learned this. In a Native American language there is a term for breathing to be eloquent. It is the same word used to become divine. Grandmother said to me, 'Breathe to be eloquent. Breathe to be God.'

Well, my little witchy heart gasped and drew back from that.

'Let's make a deal,' I thought. 'I'll work on eloquence. After all I taught public speaking and love to write and teach. But let's leave the deity thing out of this.'

How could I even think the thought, let alone share it? I still had an *us-them* relationship with the Gods. We were essentially different. I was unworthy and they were divine. Oops pardon me. Is that my Christian training peeking through? It was. I resisted accepting the whole lesson and coughed my way through journeys, studies, writing, and teaching gradually getting closer to the truth, that you and I are God.

I realized I was being as hard as an anemone rhizome, but I couldn't help it. The truth took a long time to germinate through my stubbornness. I am still drawing near. I haven't rested in it yet. I also am not 100 per cent free of my breathing issues.

However, one special journey helped.

I was travelling under the drum, seeking out information on something else entirely when Spider Woman took me up into her web spread out against the stars. She carefully showed me where to step and which hand-holds would work so I could remain untangled from the sticky lines that trap the careless. Eventually I worked my way to the center to join her for tea. I was tired. The climb had been arduous and tricky. I asked her about that but she pointed with one of her eight legs at a tightly wrapped body stuck on the web out near the perimeter. I stared a long time, realizing there were dozens of them scattered around like bodies on Mount Everest, climbers who didn't watch their step. She sipped her tea contentedly. I wondered if it was safe for human consumption. Reading my mind she looked at me with human eyes under a spider brow. I quickly drank from the cup, hoping for the best. She is after all, my grandmother. She is also a spider.

'These are people who couldn't get out of their own way so I had to take them out of the way of everyone else. Don't be like them.' I quick zoomed in on the face of the soul stealer, thinking he might be one of the bundles. I felt a flash of her impatience. He was one of her messengers. Had I not been defended against him I'd be hanging on that web with the rest of the dead wood. It was a test!

My head still spins with the implications. Those we think are evil are sent on missions from the Gods to challenge us into greater awareness. If we fail their encounters, we may be benched like a basketball player who fouls out too many times, or an athlete with a concussion who wants to play through the pain despite the danger to his future.

'Can we see anything clearly when we live on the earth?' I whined.

'Not much,' she agreed amicably and poured more tea. 'Have some cake.'

I inspected it carefully. It seemed to be ordinary pastry with raisin filling.

'Squashed flies,' she giggled. I ate it anyway. It tasted like raisins.

Despite her tricks Spider Woman remains my protector because I trust her enough to take tea with her. If my courage failed, I am sure she would put me in a package and let me twist in the wind until I grew tired of it.

'Those are like larva casings. The souls will grow wings and come out moths or butterflies when they awaken sufficiently.' She explained later. I understood whether or not one becomes a moth or a butterfly depends on one's choices.

It is also true not all of us are benched in order to learn her lessons. Some of us traverse life accepting the bitter with the better and are wiser for it. We learn that everything weaves into the tapestry. Nothing is an accident. Sometimes the truths are so big we can't see them.

In a more recent shamanic journey I discovered a different Crone sitting in a web hung in the sky, waiting for me. The setting matched my tea party with Spider Woman. I deftly climbed over the bodies and avoided the sticky trap lines.

'Shouldn't you be Spider Woman?' I asked as I sat down in the middle with the Estsanatlehi Goddess of the cycles and renewal better known as Changing Woman. Not immediately recognizing her, I heard her name as Ereshkigal and hoped I wasn't being handed off to the dark Goddess who hung her sister on a meat hook. Then I realized she did that to her sister for the same reason Spider Woman left people twisting in the wind, so they could mature.

Before I could ponder those implications, Estsanatlehi's face settled into that of the Death Crone indicating my journey question was hers to answer. Then she said I wasn't deep enough and dragged me through the center of her web into a tunnel that led to a large kiva with eight pillars supporting the dome. She hung eight silk wrapped packages on a meat hook fastened to each of the supporting structures. They represented problems clouding human vision. At the base of each support was a crystal geode useful in changing those problems of short sightedness into clarity. They were issues common to many people stuck in ordinary reality: an acceptance of things we can't do, limits; a belief in shortages, poverty; a lack of commitment to our goals and each other, excuses; devaluing ourselves and our skills, self-doubt; cluttering our minds and personal space, disorganization; expecting miracles and magic to fail, disbelief; listening to negative people, spoilers.

'So if you want to move further, follow the lines of the crystals. Discover the leys of the land. Give up on the word NO,' Changing Woman advised. She of all people knows how much things change and become new.

Spider Woman and Changing Woman often slip back and forth to become one another. Neither remains the same. Both can be young, old or in between. The Goddess in America incorporates a fluid form. Pagans are sometime chided for conflating the various European Goddesses into one Great Mother. They are not all the same, it is true. Yet the American Goddesses remind me there is a thread woven among them in spirit. They shapeshift for their pleasure and our instruction. We can sit in the web with Spider Woman and find ourselves with Estsanatlehi instead. A blink of the eye may bring her back to Spider Woman because they are the same. They are also different. They are also you and me.

Dorothy Abrams, known as Anemone Webweaver in the magical community has practiced and taught Witchcraft, paganism, and core shamanism since 1984. Co-founder of the Web PATH Center, a pagan church and teaching center in Lyons, New York USA, Dorothy has served as priestess and teacher weaving the Web of community among local pagans as they celebrate the solar and lunar sabbats. She is the author of *Identity and the Quartered Circle:*

Studies in Applied Wicca and numerous essays appearing in anthologies edited by Trevor Greenfield and by Sorita d'Este. She has published two anthologized short stories: 'Ela of Salisbury' and 'Cawing Crows and Baying Hounds'.

The Goddess and the Christian

Ave

If you visit the chapel of Mother Grove Goddess Temple in Asheville, NC, a welcome table is set outside the door. On its smooth surface is a vase of flowers, a candle, some incense and a porcelain bust of the Blessed Virgin Mary, affectionately referred to as The BVM. Come inside the chapel in December and Mary as the Goddess of Guadalupe sits in splendor on the main altar. She is surrounded by strings of bright hot peppers, tissue-paper flowers and fat squash from the temple's community garden. In mid-January, pride of place on the main altar will be given over to Brigid the Gold-Red Woman, who is both Goddess and Saint. And in March, the fat red-cob Primordial Goddess who is Mother Grove's beloved mascot will assume the high seat once again.

The ordained priestesses from the Goddess temple participate in interfaith and multifaith activities throughout the area. They are very clear about the welcoming nature of the temple – a place where people of all sorts are invited to celebrate the Divine as Female, as Mother, as Earth. That makes Mother Grove a non-denominational Goddess temple set in the midst of the southern Bible Belt. All the Female Divines: if Mother Mary or Guadalupe or the Shekinah or Sophia are the way in which a person feels the Divine Presence, that person is welcome to the table at Mother Grove.

The temple is housed on the lowest level of an old brick hospital building that currently holds offices for small non-profits and for healers that include massage therapists, reiki practitioners and herbalists. Diagonally across a busy street from this old building is another one – more beautiful, more visible. It says everything about the community that the Goddess temple is across the street from the First Baptist Church. And it says more that these two groups have a sort of working relationship, that the clergy of each know each other and are friends.

Mother Grove Temple also has a special relationship with two churches in the Episcopal Diocese. St. Mary's is up the street from Mother Grove and processions have left the Goddess temple with flowers and song and ended up a half mile away at the outdoor statue of the Blessed Virgin. She is set in a garden and in the summer, the children of the church plant lettuces and flowers at Her feet. The Goddess folks leave flowers and sweets and candles in colored votive cups. All love and adoration.

Several years ago, the Cathedral of All Souls invited Mother Grove to use its beautiful old parish hall for public rituals during cold weather. This ecumenical welcome has allowed Mother Grove to expand its programming within the walls of a tolerant and loving Christian community. At a recent diaconate ordination, priestesses from Mother Grove processed in as part of the supporting clergy for the new Episcopal deacon. They sat in reserved seating, before the gentle eyes of an icon of the Blessed Mother.

Mother. Saint. Goddess obscured. Hail, Mary, full of grace...blessed art thou amongst women.

Immaculata

As we experience the escalation of Goddess worship and its growing cultures – especially in the West – there is a kind of cold comfort in the preservation of the Divine Feminine through the machinations of Christianity. The irony, of course, is that there would have been no reason to preserve the concept of the Divine gendered as female if the Abrahamic religions had not been so insistent on their God the Father. Imagine, for a moment, an alternate history in which polytheism triumphed over the empires of monotheism. With a plurality of divinities – human and non – a Goddess-shaped space would likely have continued in the national and tribal pantheons of the West.

Visualize a Trinity of Father and Mother and Sacred Child or

Mother and Son and Non-gendered Spirit of Place or Culture. It is a sort of stealth polytheism that gives breathing space for varying views of the face of the Divine. Some adherents of modern Christianity have de-gendered the Head of the Trinity, in spite of the linguistic oddity of referring to your primary deity as 'God' while insisting on the lack of gender in the male-specific noun. But turn to the 'person of Jesus' and those insisting on his historical authenticity are also assured of his maleness. As one Congregationalist instructed me, 'Jesus had a penis.' The Third Person of this triply-aspected Divine Person is a 'holy' 'spirit.' Feminist theologians will conflate this with Sophia, but the more literalists insist that this face is also male.

And the backlash to any reimagining is usually swift and often vitriolic. Of course, Jehovah/Yahweh/Allah is male – the Sky Father All Knowing, All-Loving, All-Powerful. Jesus was a Real Man – no question of gender-bending there. And the Mystery that is the Indwelling Spirit of the Divine – a being that could be easily de-gendered – must also be muscular and decidedly comfortably male.

Him, him and him. Done and dusted. Never mind that half your adherents are female and might benefit from one face of the Triple Divines that mirrors their own.

Politically speaking, it is surprisingly easy to restrict the movements, dress, manner and potential of that portion of your demographic when they are consistently informed that they are not quite made in the image of the Divine. Human, yes. But like God? Not…exactly. We've experienced millennia of the effects of such reasoning.

Theatokos

The Blessed Virgin Mary, the Mother of God. Theodokos – the God-Bearer. She wasn't the first, of course, but she is arguably the most famous of the Divine Mothers. How could humans not find a special place in their hearts for the givers of life? The United

States stands firmly on the nonsensical and mythical foundation of Mom and Apple Pie, after all. As a species, we don't continue unless we reproduce and cultures don't progress without the ones who raise the young and keep the stories. It is certainly no wonder that some of the oldest of the great Female Divines who form the base of Western culture are parthenogenic (solo regenerators) and create the Universe through an act of self-knowledge. These beginnings offer us a vision of Female and Divine agency older than the rib-from-man tale that haunts us from Genesis. The creative power implicit in creating oneself and then the Universe is an inspiring model for woman's agency in the world. Think of Aphrodite, birthed from the foam of the sea and rising in her birthing from the primordial matrix. Or Athena (Roman Minerva) who was born, fully armored, from the top of her father's head. Athena is the goddess who first bore her self-generation in one of her ancient titles – Parthenos – and gave her name to the act of regeneration that is parthenogenesis.

First she mothers herself – this powerful and holy being. Then she births the universe, often separating it into its many parts: day and night created she them. Her act is to bear the succeeding generation of herself, to people the garden. Then she becomes the vessel for new divinity. She transforms into 'theodokas,' god-bearing. Her iconography ranges from greeting cards to the great cathedrals of Europe. Growing familiarity with the iconography of ancient Egypt has led scholars to believe that many of the 'Black Madonnas' housed in those cathedrals are actually representations of a more ancient and darker mother: Isis and her holy child Horus. Isis was only one of those holy mothers of antiquity. Almost every culture has or had one – she is often now forgotten or subsumed or cloaked.

Regina Coeli

One branch on the Abrahamic family tree did manage to hold onto some slivers of Goddess. As the Roman Empire – hardly a poster child for women's political equality – rolled through tribal and polytheist Europe, it adopted existing deities for its own uses. Sulis Minerva is the perfect example of Roman divine synthesis.

The empire's administrators arrived in a new province and explored the native religious priorities and the seats of spiritual authority. The local equivalences were identified and translated. The accepted and venerated war god became Mars and the maternal keeper of hearth and family values became Juno. Sulis, as we know from the Aquae Sulis baths and museum in Bath, became the Roman Minerva (she of wisdom and weaving), though it wasn't an exact fit. She emerged as the Romano-Celt Sulis-Minerva and the thermal springs became exquisite Roman baths. Add in the veneration of the current Emperor and make sure and pay your taxes and the new citizens of the old empire were absorbed into the fabric of the successful whole.

When that efficient and effective Pagan empire morphed into the Holy Roman Empire, the administrators – the bishops and cardinals – tweaked those protocols. It is fascinating to read the hagiographies of the early saints and to check the lists of de-canonized Catholic holy folk. In this category we'll turn our attention to Brigid of Kildare, variously known as Bride (cognate with the Welsh St. Ffraide who has similar tales), Brid, and Brighid. Her worship in Britain predates Roman and Christians. She may have traveled throughout Europe in the Proto-Indo-Europeans migrations – she certainly left her mark and her name in places like Britannia and Burgundy.

But when the Church came to Ireland, she was marvelously translated into a wonder-working, time-traveling bad-ass of a nun who played clever tricks on the local church fathers. She served as both dairymaid and daughter of a Druid and the midwife who delivered the Baby Jesus. She rose to become Ireland's Number Two Saint, with her seat at a dual-gender monastery in Cill Dara, the Church of the Oak (modern Kildare

Town, south of Dublin).

Visit that lively city – with its much-loved team the Lily Whites – and you may be fortunate to encounter the Brigadine sisters at Solas Bridhe. They have kept an eternal flame there for years and they welcome all who love Brigid – whether as Goddess or Saint. You can visit the remains of the old fire temple on the grounds of the less-old St Brigid's Church. You can see for yourself how this town holds the dynamic tension of the stealth goddesses preserved in the persons of European saints and holy women and how that is played out in a world where the word 'goddess' no longer means a Hollywood starlet with a curvy body.

At the Brigid spring, you will see revenants of worship that reach back to pre-history. Ragged clouties bear witness to spring-lore when a lesser goddess reigned supreme, offering the healing and blessing of the water as it bubbles through the earth. Goddess to holy woman to saint and back to goddess again, all the time her veneration is kept by the women of a certain place, linking the honorifics in simple and homely patterns of connection with the Divines as experienced through life.

Those of us who share a love of history know that some of the first slaves in the Americas were not African, but Irish. This helps us understand Brigid's other persona, as Maman Brigitte, wife of the dashing Baron Samedi, Mother of the Dead. The synthesis is comfortable for those who honor this lwa – there is a song for her that includes this: 'Brigitte, she comes from England,' acknowledging her deeper roots.

Rosary

Maria. Marie. Maris. Stella Maris.

The next step for the Church was a simple and effective technique in which any native goddess was Mary. The beauty of this was that a direct experience of Goddess did not exclude a Christian believer from the fold of a male-god dominated religion. These apparitions of the Holy Mother were suitably rebranded and celebrated. Care was taken that she never overstepped the bounds of power. Her job in these appearances was to act as justification for the Christian overlay and she was charged to bring comfort, to aid in healing. She is seen in Lourdes, in Medjugorje, in Knock, in Fatima. Here in the Americas, we know her best as the Blessed Mother Guadalupe, with her miracle of roses in the winter. These Marys' message is one of love and faithfulness and hope in the face of despair.

Good women who were outstanding credits to their culture and the Church were often Christened with 'Mary' and sometimes went on to be declared saints. Brigid is often referred to as the 'Mary of the Gaels.'

Mother Mary continues to bear the older remnants in her traditional colors: the blue of sky and sea and the white of seafoam reflect the sea goddesses of Middle Eastern and Mediterranean countries. She wears a crown of stars as befits the Queen of Heaven. One of the most universal symbols of female power, both divine and human, twists near her feet in the form of a snake.

The BVM is recognized – and has been for some time – as co-redemptrix with her Holy Son. Even the Catholics don't assert that you can go to the Mother instead of the Son, but they acknowledge her as a significant part of redeeming sinful humankind from their perilous condition. She moves one step closer to her old authority, her old place in the realm of religious power.

Benedicta

Returning, returning. Here at the end, we come back to the notion of the unveiling of the Goddess and how she has been obscured in the belly of Christianity, awaiting her own time of rebirth. She has come down to modern secular Americans in Christmas decorations, in children's jolly songs about the birth of the Holy

Child. She has been venerated in extraordinary visual and performing arts throughout the ages since she was translated from goddess of place to Queen of Heaven to Mother Mary and the female saints and back, at last, full circle.

There's a funny story about Christians, the BVM and the influx of immigrants from Spanish-speaking lands to the south. Most of the immigrants are Catholics and when they first started arriving, their English wasn't very strong. They naturally turned to Catholic churches for a familiarity of setting and worship style, which disturbed some of the Protestant churches.

One of them came up with a clever idea and others followed suit. They went to garden centers and bought concrete Mary statues for their front lawns. They gave them pride of place and some even planted around them to make them look like long-standing denizens of those little churches. I don't know if any of the new immigrants fell for the ruse, but it was a boon to garden centers and it moved the Beloved and Divine Mother once step closer to those little Protestant churches.

The re-emergence of Goddess worship in modern American culture owes its strength and diversity to the patchwork quilt that is the United States. There is a little square of that quilt that holds the Holy Mother as She stands humbly in the hearts of Christian people. Her strength, Her resilience and Her crooked path forward and back through time to the Goddesses are another of Her gifts – and Their gifts – to the people who love and worship Them.

H. Byron Ballard is a writer, teacher and ritualist in Asheville, NC. She has been a featured presenter at Pagan Unity Festival, Sacred Space Conference, Pagan Spirit Gathering, FaerieCon and Southeast Wise Women Herbal Conference. She can be reached at www.myvillagewitch.com.

The Goddess and the Psychologist

I was a lonely child. For a variety of reasons, I tended toward the solitary rather than surround myself with a host of neighborhood children my own age. As a young child, I had friends. They just weren't of the corporeal variety. For a while, I was accompanied by a brontosaurus. She was lovely and gentle, but she wasn't very good at hopscotch. She couldn't throw marker stones very well and she tended to make a muck of the carefully drawn chalk lines. So we parted ways and I befriended Artemis. She walked to school with me and gave most excellent guidance on those school age troubles that can seem insurmountable. And She was a fantastic hopscotch player. With Her gift for precision and timing, She had terrific aim and challenged me to up my game.

These were innocent imaginations born out of a child's need for connection, but they served a significant purpose. In adulthood, I (along with so many others) found *Goddesses in Everywoman: A New Psychology of Women* by Jean Shinoda Bolen (New York: Harper & Row, 1985.) It illuminated and anchored something in me that I had felt innately as a child. These are not characters simply found in stories from times long past, serving to entertain and amuse. These are not tales that carry little relevance to modern society and culture. The stories and the characters around whom these myths swirl are archetypal and timeless. They reflect aspects of ourselves and can serve to guide, encourage, and support us. The Goddess is found in psychology and She has much to teach us.

The Goddess Meets the Doctor

Psychology is seen as the study of human behavior and mental processes, but a strict translation of the word belies a very different function. Psychology comes from the Latin 'logia', which means 'the study of', and the Latinized version of the

Greek 'psyche', which means 'soul'. The name reverberates with the myth of Psyche, a mortal woman so beautiful that she evoked Aphrodite's jealousy. Hers is a complex, multi-layered story. She incurs the wrath of a Goddess which, ironically leads to her finding love, but which also leads to a crisis of faith. She must undertake trials to prove herself, including descent to the Underworld, which leads to the reclaiming of her love and culminates in her achieving Divine status as the Goddess of the Soul. The word 'psychology' thus implies within its true definition that a psychological process involves undertaking the deep inner journey to reclaim that which makes our heart whole. It is the work of the Soul and it requires the courage to step into the challenge.

Myth also holds that the first physician was Asklepios. The rod of Asklepios, the staff entwined with two snakes, stands as the symbol of medicine even today. Son of Apollo and a mortal woman, Koronis, he learned the healing arts from the centaur Chiron and became a healer of such great skill that he was able to raise the dead. The cult of Asklepios rose to great popularity by 350BCE and the ancient world was dotted with asklepeia, healing temples dedicated to him. Individuals flocked to the asklepeia to undergo the process of dream incubation. The dream that was visited onto the seeker was said to hold the key to the cure. Thus, via the introduction of dream interpretation to facilitate healing, the doctor Asklepios was also arguably the first psychologist.

The more contemporary roots for the correlation between the Goddess and psychology can be found in the work of another doctor. Carl G. Jung, founder of analytical psychology (also known as Jungian or depth psychology) introduced the concept of the 'collective unconscious,' which was both revolutionary and shocking to a large faction of his peers and colleagues. The concept of the personal unconscious had already been established by Freud and was well-accepted. The idea that there is a storehouse of all our personal experiences and particular emotions that drive us to react or respond in certain ways was at the foundation of the burgeoning field of psychology. Jung took this idea further to present that there is a storehouse of experiences that are common to all human beings. The common elements contained within this storehouse are called archetypes. 'Mother,' 'Lover,' and 'Child' are a few of the many archetypes we all contain. Each and every one of us contains the 'shape' of the archetype waiting to be filled by our experience, although what that experience specifically looks like is going to be different for each of us. Joseph Campbell, best known for his work in comparative mythology, brought the scope of archetypes to a wider cultural arena. He saw similar themes and characters in the myths and stories of cultures all across the globe, thus identifying the archetypal themes that have been present throughout history for all peoples.

James Hillman, who studied at, then guided studies for the C.G. Jung Institute in Zurich, recognized the aforementioned disconnect between modern psychology and the work of the soul. As the founder of archetypal psychology, he strove to reintegrate Psyche or soul into psychology (*Re-visioning Psychology*. New York: Harper & Row, 1975). He saw psychological disorders as 'soul suffering' and, evoking remembrances of Asklepios, presented that the soul attempts to communicate its pain (and thus the key to its healing) through myth and metaphor.

Hillman's direct connection between soul, psychology and the archetypes blasted open the door for the Goddess. The first seven Goddesses to step squarely into the therapy room through Bolen's work (ibid, page 14), were Demeter as mother, Persephone as daughter, Hera as wife, Aphrodite as lover, Artemis as sister and competitor, Athena as strategist, and Hestia as hearthkeeper. They were presented as archetypes that resonate particularly with women's experiences. This was not just a step in another direction for psychology. In a discipline that had been largely dominated by men, the arrival of the Goddesses was informed by and expanded upon political activism. Born out of the particular flavor of 1960s' feminism (as Venus emerging from the foam), it was a clear message that the psychology of women has its own shape. To heal the suffering in a woman's soul, it is necessary to access and activate the archetypes that speak directly to a woman's experience. And these would be the Goddesses.

When the soul is included in the picture, the line between psychology and spirituality is very thin indeed. The headstrong, rebel children of Germaine Greer's *The Female Eunuch* (New York: McGraw-Hill, 1971) and Merlin Stone's *When God was a Woman* (originally published as *The Paradise Papers: The Suppression of Women's Rites*. London: Virago, 1976) were the women and men who blurred this line completely. With each passing decade, resting on the work of many in the areas of sociology, archeology, politics, spirituality, and psychology, it became increasingly evident that the cornerstone to creating a solid foundation of personal empowerment and wholeness for women must include an experience that reflects the Divine Feminine within.

Interestingly, what seems to have transpired in the decades between the 1970s and now is that, as women have begun to turn more and more to the Goddess in order to find positive, affirming self-reflection, so have the Goddesses moved into a different sphere of interpretation. This may be best illustrated in the case of Lilith who has been portrayed through much of history as the part-bird, part-snake demoness who preyed on pregnant women and babies, instilling terror and prompting powerful protective action in the form of magical inscriptions against Her. Thousands of years have seen Her hated and vilified and yet, in the past few decades, many women have begun to see Her as the symbol for strength and autonomy that refuses to bow under the patriarchal yoke. What began as accessing the Goddess tales for wisdom has taken a turn toward revisioning the tales to glean the nuggets that may lie buried beneath the patriarchal overlay. As stated so eloquently by Jhenah Telyndru: 'The renewed concept of woman as sacred has truly transformed mindsets, dissolved outdated paradigms of a woman's place, reset our search for human purpose, and refined our concept of the nature of the Divine.' (*Avalon Within: A Sacred Journey of Myth, Mystery, and Inner Wisdom*. Woodbury, MN: Llewellyn Publications, 2010. Pg 2.)

The Goddess Grasps the Rod

There is a particular aspect of feminine energy that lends itself to a more expansive approach to self-awareness and healing than has been experienced in the centuries since medicine moved from the carefully gathered herbs of the wise woman to the insular medical communities of the first monastic educational institutions. More and more, as our approach to healing in the West acknowledges a holistic approach, the unidirectional rod of Asklepios is becoming multi-dimensional.

What becomes interesting about working with the Goddess from a psychological perspective is that we are not as tied to remaining within the parameters of a particular pantheon. In a spiritual practice, we may choose to work solely with the deities within a specific tradition, but with the psychological focus on archetypal energies, it is the core 'flavor' of the archetype that is significant, rather than the adherence to cultural cohesion. To gain deeper self-awareness of motherhood, we can look to Gaia, Cybele, Tellus, Isis, Hathor, Demeter, Frigg, Nerthus, Danu, Rhiannon, Branwen, or Ceridwen. Some Goddesses who provide more complex and conflicted reflections of motherhood are Hera, Arianrhod, and even Aphrodite. For each aspect of our lives, there are a multitude of Goddesses who can help us to understand what may be informing our experience and guide us to respond with greater acceptance and conscious choice. This multi-dimensional approach opens up an infinite number of creative ways to access inner truth and self-knowledge.

The Inner Goddess Map

The question of who we are is not easily nor quickly answered. The fact is, we respond differently to different circumstances and in various areas of our lives. Working with the Goddess in the context of psychology is actually the work of discovering which face of the Goddess shows up when. One benefit from working with a myriad pantheons is the ability to discern nuances between the various faces of the Divine Feminine, thus creating a finely-tuned inner map. Many women find themselves involved in the roles of mother, lover, and professional. However, the inner triad of Mother Hathor – Lover Aphrodite – Professional Brigit has a completely different energy than the inner triad of Mother Hera – Lover Blodeuwedd – Professional Freya. Rather than try to fit into something that does not resonate within, coming to better know the Goddesses who appear in these areas of our lives helps us to accept the unique Goddess combinations that make us who we are. We can begin to appreciate both our complexity and our diversity.

Goddess Dialoguing

Voice dialoguing is a useful technique used in Transpersonal Psychology, which works on the basic premise that all behaviors in which we engage are aimed at protecting us, regardless of how misguided and destructive the result. Actions that serve to create challenges, difficulties, or disasters in our lives are unconscious reactions stemming from unresolved pain and unhealthy beliefs. These actions are motivated by 'subpersonalities' – recognizable roles we take on that cause us to behave in predictable ways. For example, the 'caretaker subpersonality' will always neglect her own needs, prioritizing the needs of everyone around her, unconsciously trying to ensure that these others will remain dependent on her and she will never be left or abandoned. It is a protective action. It shields the caretaker from the possibility of devastating loss. Caretakers are helpful, loving, and supportive, but the cost is often exhaustion, lack of self-esteem, and sometimes resentment.

Voice dialoguing externalizes the subpersonality, allowing us to have a conversation much in the same way we would with another person. When working with the caretaker subpersonality, one could imagine sitting across from one's self in that particular guise, asking questions about what 'she' is afraid of, what caused 'her' to come into being, how this way of acting is having a negative impact, and what might be a healthier way of showing heartfelt care. This technique acknowledges that we do not want to eliminate that which is positive in our lives. We want to transmute pain into empowerment.

It is exactly the same when working with Goddesses. A Hathor mother may give endlessly, to the point of self-negation. Goddess dialogue may reveal the roots of a neglected childhood and the unconscious determination to never inflict that pain on her own children. A healed Hathor may result in a mother who is able to meet the needs of her children while being able to nurture herself as well. Goddess dialoguing is a method through which we can access the positive, empowered attributes of the Divine Feminine.

The Goddess as Higher Self

In Transpersonal Psychology, the Higher Self is recognized as that aspect of self which reflects the best in us. It is the personal experience of the Divine that is objective, discerning, and wise. It is not informed by our pain nor the wounds from our past. Rather, it sees our old wounds as part of the big picture of our lives, providing the key to our gifts, our strengths, and our unique expression in the world.

When we have recognized which Goddesses are present in the different areas of our lives and when we have reclaimed their specific qualities to support emotional and psychological health, we have integrated Higher Self with Divine Feminine. We can anticipate what may be challenging in situations we face and consciously activate the Goddess who will best meet that situation. We may activate Maat when caught in a dispute. We may enlist Arianrhod when asking for a raise. We may embody Kwan Yin when comforting a friend. This is not 'becoming the Goddess.' Jung took particular pains to clarify that it is important to never 'become the archetype.' Archetypal energy is too expansive to be contained in one individual. Rather, this is the recognition that we reflect many faces of the Goddess within and that, as complex beings, we will reflect a different face depending on the time, place, environment, and situation.

The Goddess Beyond Therapy

Psychology has gone through many changes in the hundred years or so since it has been a formalized practice. What was once relegated to the office of a professional has found a myriad forms of expression in recent years. Revisiting Psyche once again, if psychology is the 'study of the soul', many individuals are engaging in this process in ways simply not available in decades past.

Inspired by the book by Anita Diamant (*The Red Tent*. New York: Wyatt Book for St. Martin's, 1997), The Red Tent Movement holds the vision of creating safe space for women in which they can release, at least for a moment, the roles they feel obliged to hold in the world. These roles, as outlined above, are necessary, but they do not always reflect a woman's deep, inner truth and her personal experience of herself. Touching a need in women, Red Tents are cropping up all over the world. Time and time again, in these Tents, regardless of whether it is the explicit intent or not, women are afforded the opportunity to connect to the truth of their Spirits and in this, they reflect the face of the Goddess.

As oracles become more and more popular, there is a plethora of fantastic Goddess oracle decks available, which allow for daily connection with many Goddesses from various cultures. Use of Goddess oracles is a beautiful way in which to experience the Goddess as Higher Self. When we trust the process, it is a simple matter to meditate upon how the Goddess who came to us that day is exactly the right Goddess to guide us in whatever situation we see before us. If facing a dispute, the appearance of Maat would give us a very different message than an appearance of Pele or Athena or Hekate. Working with Goddess oracles greatly expands our range of responses and encourages us to look beyond the obvious surface to seek that which we may have inadvertently overlooked.

The Goddesses have also walked out of the myths of old into the stories of now. Campbell saw myths as integral to teaching us about how to embrace this human existence. He held that all stories are teaching stories and, slowly but surely, we are seeing the appearance of the Goddesses in novels such as Elizabeth Cunningham's *The Return of the Goddess* (Barrytown, NY: Station Hill, 1992), Staci Backauskas' *The Fifth Goddess* (Atlantic Highlands, NJ: Jai Creations, 1999), or P. C. Cast's *Goddess Summoning* series. What makes the new stories different from myths is that they show us the Goddesses in relation to ourselves. They are not stories about the Goddesses. They are stories about women who experience the arrival of the Divine upon their doorsteps in surprising and unexpected ways, leaving them forever changed. They reflect the human experience and teach us how to align ourselves when we recognize the Goddesses' impact on ourselves and our lives.

I first met the Goddess as a lonely child at a hopscotch game. These days, I am blessed to have many friends. That little girl has transformed into a near-crone with a full heart, but Artemis has never left my side. As in childhood, She has informed many of my significant decisions in adulthood and serves as the inspiration for much of my work. But She has been joined by an abundant host of Goddesses, each one of them with much to share about living a life with Soul. The study that bears Psyche's name has been enlivened by the introduction of the Goddess – in all Her faces.

Tiffany Lazic is a spiritual psychotherapist and founder of The Hive and Grove Centre for Holistic Wellness (www.hiveand-grove.ca). She is the creator of several self-development programs, including 'The Spiritual Language of the Divine' and author of *The Great Work: Self-Knowledge and Healing Through the Wheel of the Year* (Llewellyn, 2015).

The Goddess and the Witch

When I volunteered to pen this chapter on the relationship between the goddess and the witch in America, I did so under the ill-conceived notion that it would be a quick and simple chapter to complete. After all, goddesses and witches go hand-in-hand, do they not? And to put an American spin on the topic should have been easy enough – we tend to put a hearty sprinkling of Americana on just about everything we undertake. As it turns out, however, we can't even agree on the definition of 'witch', much less on the practices and beliefs of those witches! There is quite a bit of healthy (and not-so-healthy) debate out there that attempts to define and classify witchcraft in America. The simple truth is that American witchcraft and goddess worship are as vast and diverse as the land itself. Goddesses from all corners of the world, and across the depths of time, have been welcomed within these borders. And the craft itself is in a constant state of motion, evolving and transforming as it rebels against the limitations of definition.

Although it's safe to assume that witches, in some manner, have always existed in America, modern witchcraft did not emerge until the 1960s. When Rosemary and Raymond Buckland introduced Gardnerian Wicca to the country, they found an eager audience in the growing counterculture movement. The questioning of old values and religious systems left an entire generation searching for life's answers in new and alternative ways. For many, witchcraft and Wicca provided an environment where spirituality could thrive without the constraints of traditional Western religions. For others, witchcraft melded with ongoing activism and the issues of the day – a renewed eagerness to connect with and protect the natural world, gender equality, and a desire for peaceful solutions over violent reactions. The 60s provided a fertile environment for witchcraft to expand rapidly throughout the United States, and it remains one of the fastest growing religious movements in America today.

Almost as soon as Gardnerian Wicca landed on the shores of the United States, it began to evolve and transform into a myriad interpretations and practices. While some American witches maintained Gerald Gardner's form of witchcraft absolutely, others sought to revise it or rejected it outright. New traditions began flowering throughout the nation: Dianic, Feri, Reclaiming, and countless others. Whether embraced or simply inspiring a renewed interest in pre-Christian religions, British Traditional Wicca, of which Gardnerian Wicca is a pivotal member, became the springboard for the development of modern American Wicca and witchcraft. But one aspect of Gardner's craft remained almost universal – veneration of the goddess.

At the roots of Gardnerian Wicca, and subsequently early modern American witchcraft, was the belief in a duality of deities. For many Americans, especially women, this was a tantalizing aspect that initially drew them into the craft. Gardner referred to two opposite, yet equal, forces known simply as the Horned God and Mother Goddess. It was the balance and union of these two that, according to Gardner, was the basis of all creation. The Goddess, sometimes also referred to as Aradia, is seen as the divine feminine incarnate. In witchcraft, there is no denial of the inherent power of the feminine as is often the case in other Western religions. The goddess does not stand above or below the god, but on a dais of equal importance. American witches readily embraced this benevolent Mother Goddess, finding personal empowerment through her.

By the 1970s, American witches began to increasingly modify or effectively abandon Gardnerian Wicca. As they explored the craft and began forging their own personal connections to the Divine Goddess, differing perspectives as to the nature of the goddess and divinity began to evolve. Certainly there were witches who observed (and still observe) Gardner's Wicca as it originated, but many more began to seek their own spiritual answers and paths to the goddess.

If we were to gather a group of twenty witches and ask each of them what their understanding of the goddess was, we'd likely receive twenty very different answers. If we also asked those witches to put a name to the goddess, we would undoubtedly receive a variety of responses. Some would explain that there is only one goddess while others would embrace a variety, perhaps even from different pantheons. Like many aspects of witchcraft, individual interpretations of divinity are developed through devotion, study, and personal experience.

Although witchcraft is intrinsically polytheistic, many witches recognize a single goddess and that all other goddesses are simply aspects or manifestations of her. They may give her a name, or they may refer to her simply as the Goddess or the Lady. For these witches, one goddess and one god are the genesis of all creation. They are the sum of all other deities, pre-eminent and yet equal. In this interpretation, the Great Goddess embodies the entirety of the feminine creative spirit and is often shown as the triple aspect of maiden, mother, and crone.

Other witches embrace a myriad goddesses as separate individuals each with unique personalities and associations. A witch may honor the goddesses and gods of a single pantheon, or she (or he) may work with deities from a number of cultures. Often a particular deity will be called on that fits the specific needs of the witch. The United States is often referred to as a 'melting pot' of peoples, and the American witch often uses that rich cultural mosaic to call upon many diverse goddesses. It's important to note, however, that these witches do not see themselves as having power over the goddess. Instead, they work to develop relationships and partnerships with the goddesses to assist them in both their spiritual and mundane lives.

Within witchcraft there is also the concept of a point of creation beyond that of even the supreme Goddess and God.

Gardner referred to this force as 'Prime Mover', but it has also been referred to as The One, Dryghten, or star goddess. For some, this highest power is considered the seat of creation, an unknowable force that gives birth to all that was, is, or ever will be. This includes the goddess and god. These witches recognize this being, but do not worship it. Others believe it possible to nurture a relationship with the Highest and that she should be included in worship. As in other areas of witchcraft, belief in this highest power is deeply personal. Some embrace the star goddess in one form or another while others exclude her from their ideals completely.

Regardless of whether a witch believes that all goddesses are one goddess or if she (or he) believes in many unique goddesses, the majority share a belief that all things in the universe are connected. Witches recognize that nature is composed of a delicate blend of spiritual energy and physical substance. This interconnection can be visualized as a vast web spun by the goddess and permeating all things. When one strand of the web is disturbed, the effects ripple throughout the entirety of the universe. Each action has a shared consequence. For some, the earth itself is seen as a physical embodiment of the Mother Goddess and therefore worthy of praise and reverence. Because witches recognize the goddess as both a part of nature and its creator, many American witches are adamant environmentalists.

As American witches forged their own paths to the goddess and developed their own understanding of her, witchcraft continued to expand and evolve throughout the nation. By the 1990s, thousands of Americans were practicing witchcraft in covens or in private. Because of the lack of universal theology, when witches were unable to find a tradition that suited them, they simply created a new one. A spectrum began to develop that melded historical inspiration with modern need and creativity. At one end, reconstructionists attempted to faithfully recreate the ancient pagan religions and traditional witchcraft of pre-

Christian Europe. At the opposite end, eclectics brewed up their own witchcraft with elements from multiple cultures and beliefs. And, although vastly different in practice, the goddess remained the common thread that connected witches across the nation.

For the reconstructionists, issues developed fairly early with Gardner's history of witchcraft and the development of Wicca. Many began to point out historical inaccuracies in his account and in those of other early modern witches. Although rejected, Gardner's witchcraft did inspire many to begin researching and resurrecting ancient beliefs. America is home to a multitude of witches working to recreate the practices of specific ethnic groups. For these witches, folklore and traditional literature meld with historic and archaeological evidence in the attempts to accurately replicate the traditions of the ancients. Hellenic reconstructionists strive to uphold the practices of the ancient Greeks. Kemetics are recreating the customs of the Egyptians. Celtic reconstructionists focus on the lore of the ancient people of northern and western Europe. Witches within these traditions, and many others, look for historically accurate ways to connect with and honor the goddesses. Festivals and rites are recreated, but may be often tempered with modern sensibilities. For example, ritual sacrifice was a widespread practice throughout the ancient world and was used to celebrate both goddesses and gods in various pantheons. Today, reconstructionist witches typically acknowledge this practice as a part of their past, but find other, nonviolent, ways to incorporate those rituals into their tradition. Reconstructionist witchcraft often transforms itself as new historical data emerges. Instead of rejecting information that may seem to contradict their picture of the past, reconstructionists welcome changes and see new developments simply as a means to better recreate the practices of the past.

As an American, it is not uncommon for a family to have lost or forgotten its ancestral heritage throughout the generations. While there are communities all across the nation that celebrate

distinct heritages, many are left with no family histories or traditions that can be directly traced back to an ancestral homeland.
My own family is a prime example of this. There exists no tales
or traditions within my family that are obviously connected with
any culture other than that of the southern United States. Because
of this, many American witches are left longing for a connection
with the past. It is not uncommon for a witch to spend a great
deal of time and energy researching and testing her (or his) DNA
in an attempt to discover family origins. The concept of a
'homeland' is an important one in witchcraft. Early Europeans
believed that their goddesses and gods resided within the land
itself. When these peoples would move to a new location, the
deities were taken as well by creating a connection between their
native lands and the new home. Beneath the umbrella of reconstructionism, we can find American witches actively working to
marry the goddesses of their ancestral homelands with the
goddesses native to the American soil. A witch with ancestral ties
to Ireland might invite the goddess Aine to inhabit the land on
which she (or he) now resides. That witch might create rituals or
sacred space for the goddess Aine while also connecting with the
goddesses of the native peoples of the area. For example, if a
witch lives on land once inhabited by the Cherokee people, she
(or he) may also invite Grandmother Spider to join Aine and
would work to develop and foster a relationship with both.
Traditions and practices from both cultures would be observed
while new ones combining the energies were developed, making
this practice a type of eclectic reconstructionism.

Although reconstructionism has seen considerable growth in
recent years, eclectic witchcraft is overwhelmingly prevalent in
the United States. The nature of America itself lends quite well to
eclecticism. Within the American cauldron are boundless
numbers of nationalities, cultures, faiths, beliefs, and customs for
the eclectic witch to draw from. This form of witchcraft is highly
personalizable and many eclectic witches feel as though they

were called by a specific goddess or goddesses. For every possible circumstance and situation, there is a goddess somewhere that can be called upon for assistance. Eclectics are comfortable with working and developing relationships with goddesses from across the world. An eclectic American witch may have on her altar figures of Isis, Kali, Brigid, Astarte, and the Hopi goddess Kokyan. As the witch grows in her (or his) practice, those goddesses may change. Eclecticism makes allowances for the growth and evolution of the witch. For many Americans born into traditional, structured Western religions, this freedom to form and reform beliefs is often what draws a person initially to witchcraft.

According to a recent poll, there are currently more than a million practicing pagans (which includes both witches and Wiccans) in the United States. They are predominantly college educated, middle class people living in urban areas on the West and East coasts. And, while many enjoy working within a coven or group, a great number of witches practice their craft alone. Whether by choice or necessity, solitary practitioners in the United States are believed to outnumber their European counterparts. Although in recent years a visible shift has occurred in the United States away from Christianity, most of the country remains deeply rooted in the faith. For witches living in deeply religious regions, such as the American Bible Belt, coming out as a witch can be a dangerous proposition even today. These witches have found a multitude of ways to incorporate their magical crafts into their everyday lives in a way that is practically invisible to the average person. They practice folk magic, kitchen witchery, and hedge witchery. They may adorn their altars with flowers and crystals as offerings to the goddesses instead of goddess iconography. They create and perform their own initiations and rituals. They may look to traditional witchcraft lineages for guidance or establish their own system wholly. Other solitary practitioners simply choose to practice their craft on their own while yet others find that their rural environments make it difficult to find and connect with other witches.

American witchcraft is undeniably a complex and diverse craft. It is as multi-faceted as the witches who practice it. But beneath all the various branches, the goddess remains the root of witchcraft. The craft may have arrived, in its modern sense, from the British Isles, but it has absorbed a deeply American essence as it has grown. For many, the goddess and witchcraft represent the kind of idealistic freedom that the very country was built upon. It is the freedom to seek out divinity in a personal way, without the need for accepted dogma and rigid hierarchies. The goddess does not demand a specific belief or action. She is not greedy nor vain. Like any mother, she seeks simply to guide her children along their own paths. America, like all countries, has its own unique energies. Those energies are both young and ancient, stable and transitionary. The American witch learns to interact with these energies and to combine them with the infinite energies of the goddess.

Undoubtedly, I have only begun to unravel the intricacies of the American witch and goddess within these few pages. There are many branches of the craft that I have not even touched upon in this chapter. An exhaustive look would easily fill an entire tome. And therein lies the inherent beauty of witchcraft. Each witch creates a new chapter in witchcraft's Book of Shadows. Each writes her own story into the pages. And permeating every word is the love of the goddess.

Laurie Martin-Gardner is a reiki master-teacher, author, and artisan, Laurie is a lifelong student of myth and magick. She currently has two books available and frequently writes for several spiritual magazines.

Part 4

The Contemporary Goddess

From Marilyn to Maleficent: Pop Goes the Goddess

The *Pocket Webster School & Office Dictionary* defines a goddess as '1. A female deity. 2. a woman of superior charm and excellence.'(311). While this is a simple definition, it comes nowhere near where we, as a society, have defined what truly is a 'goddess.' From historical texts to modern-day movies, a goddess has been portrayed as both, as well as a combination of both, definitions. Modern renditions of age-old lore give us illustrations as well as descriptions of women of beauty, described as goddesses, who could charm men with their grace, good looks, and personality. A more modern interpretation could lead one to believe that a goddess is simply a beautiful woman. Popular culture has lead us to look at the more superficial definition of goddess and this has led to an obscured view of what Pagans, Wiccans, witches, and other non-Christians truly revere. I intend to look at the positive and negative influences of popular culture on goddess worship and what goddesses are in general.

The neo-paganism movement has grown in size by leaps and bounds. Goddess worship is more mainstream now. A wider acceptance, quite possibly due to the internet and easier access to books and learning materials as well as a fascination with the supernatural in Hollywood, has made exposure to this 'new' old religion reach farther and wider than any other time. Bringing the Goddess into the modern light, making her more mainstream, has brought her love and warmth back to many who never knew she existed. Women and men have created websites and Facebook groups dedicated to certain kinds of goddess worship. New Age stores, carrying jewelry, tools, books, magazines, and newspaper-style readers, provide a wealth of contacts and sources seekers can utilize to learn more about their chosen goddess or spiritual path. Going into a Barnes and Noble branch, or any other book store that is secular, you will find it generally hosts a New Age section that combines witchcraft, Wicca, shamanism, astrology, and a host of other spiritual paths' reading material as well as books on the supernatural. Acceptance of this ever-growing belief system is more prevalent in literature, television, and in the movies now than it has been since the rise of Christianity and other organized religions.

Modern and relatively easy research methods, such as typing 'goddess' into a chosen search engine on the internet, provide a host of websites, books, movies, television shows, and articles all about goddesses. Looking for pictures of a goddess and you are sure to find pictures of women with ethereal beauty, surrounded by whatever element or animal or natural setting they are connected with and unless otherwise indicated, they are never old, never ugly, never lacking in mystery. You will even find the traditional garb of Greek and Roman gods and goddesses for sale as costumes, white robes and togas, flowing fabrics, tutorials for hair flowing wildly or pulled into a beautiful cascade of gleaming curls and tresses. There are even make-up styles and tutorials, accentuated eye make-up, long full lashes, shimmer and glitter. The popular culture of goddesses, the interest, and the mysteries, the interpretations of what they are and what they should be are plastered all over the internet, in movies, and in books. This lends even more to the modernized interpretation of goddess rather than the more traditional interpretation of a goddess being a female deity that is worshipped and revered rather than read about and watched on television.

Movies have done an excellent job of helping to provide a modern definition of a goddess without truly defining THE Goddess. With the more recent film focus on Marvel comics, the introduction of the Norse gods and goddesses, particularly Thor, Odin, and Freya, have brought mythology and god and goddess worship to a place where we can put a face to the name. Freya, the mother of Thor in the movie, 'Thor: The Dark World', is portrayed by Renea Russo. She is tall, blonde, and blue-eyed. She is grace and beauty and wisdom and love. She is strength and fearlessness. She is nobility and self-sacrificing. She is a warrior goddess queen. This goddess, who was brought to life on the silver screen, is not unlike what most women want to be seen as and remembered as by all who know them. The books about Percy Jackson give life to Greek gods and goddesses, bringing back the demigods and demigoddesses to bring to life the stories of Athena, Medusa, and Aphrodite. Disney has even begun to give a new face to a goddess with its rendition the Sleeping Beauty story, told from the side of the supposed villainess, Maleficent. She was the protector, the caretaker, the guardian of the enchanted forest and she embodied innocence and intelligence and, yet again, beauty. When part of her power was stolen, she still remained, albeit begrudgingly, the protagonist and was given the name 'Godmother' by little Aurora. Popular culture has managed to take the villainous 'goddesses', known for their evil ways and treacherous acts, and it has reformed them to fit into societal standards of what is good and evil, sinister and innocent. Her inner beauty took a beating, but Maleficent survived to thrive as a goddess on our movie and television screens.

Beauty is seen as a commodity in our society. Beauty is respected, it is power. It isn't uncommon to hear in everyday conversation a beautiful woman being described as a goddess. In the 1995 movie, 'French Kiss', the character Charlie describes the woman he is leaving his fiancé, Kate, for as a 'god-dess', with emphasis placed on the end of the word. When you finally catch a glimpse of the woman, Juliette, he has left Kate for, you see that Charlie has been simply enraptured by her youth and beauty. Her looks were her power and that gave her the ability to be referred to as a goddess. Sure, her personality may be one of charm, elegance, and grace; however, her character is very two dimensional, with little time given to flesh out her character. Take Marilyn Monroe, certainly a beautiful woman, who was also considered a mortal goddess, lest we forget a true goddess is immortal. The 2007 book, *Goddess: The Secret Lives of Marilyn Monroe* by Anthony Summers, gives her the moniker of goddess in the title, proclaiming to all and sundry that her beauty and fame were what made her a goddess. But what made her truly like a goddess? She was a drug addict, a mistress, a young woman corrupted by the ills of Hollywood and who tragically lost her life. What traits made her worthy of the name held for a divine female? Angelina Jolie, famous not only for her acting talent and beauty, but also her grace, humanitarian acts, and philanthropic efforts has also been given the moniker goddess. But does this take away from the true and intended religious name of goddess? Does giving the name goddess, or the description of a woman as a goddess, sully the reverence goddess worshiping religions and spiritual believers have? These are questions that can only be answered by the individual.

In an era where self-help books reign supreme, one can find books everywhere telling women they can learn how to bring out their 'inner goddess.' An excellent example of this would be the book, *The Modern Goddess' Guide to Life: How to be Absolutely Divine on a Daily Basis* by Francesca de Grandis. Yes, an inner goddess needs to be recognized, nurtured, and loved. Every woman contains within her a spark of divinity that needs recognition and nurturing. But the commerciality of this now very common practice comes with what? The cost of divinity? At the cost of possibly cheapening how a goddess should be considered, is the modernization of what a goddess truly is versus what popular culture has made her really a good thing? Can we, as goddess worshippers, stand by and allow the divinity drained from our image of the Goddess to be replaced with popular cultural definitions of what a goddess should be? Again, these are questions that can only be answered by the individual.

One could say goddess worship has been slightly trivialized and twisted by the dabblers, with much thanks to pop culture.

The popularity of gods and goddesses, made so by the rise of the movement and the accessibility of information has brought about a wave of partial practitioners. The half-hearted practices by those who want to be 'different' rather than true to their own path sully the practice of goddess worship and, often, they will engage in unrealistic rituals they found on the internet and/or spout facts and information that they feel will make them relevant to the group they want to join without having the deeper understanding of what it is they are engaging in. Those who take what they want from bits of information here and there without truly understanding what it means to worship THE Goddess or even A goddess cheapen what is important: reverence and under-standing, respect for the Goddess and what she represents and what she might provide if your petitioning falls in her favor. We can completely see the influence of movies and television shows in this. With movies like 'The Craft' and 'Practical Magic', television shows like 'Sabrina: The Teenage Witch' and 'Charmed', Wicca and witchcraft, both of which contain some form of goddess worship, society is given a very Hollywood look at what both practices are not but what many believe they are. Many do not understand that goddess worship is not about spells and clothing and the kind of jewelry you wear, but under-standing what the Goddess, whatever goddess you are paying reverence to at the time of your worship and petitioning, repre-sents and what can be done to curry her favor, show her respect, and to treat her as you would a matriarch of your family. To worship the Goddess is to worship the Mother and all that she entails.

Thanks to popular culture, many people think that those who worship the Goddess are either crunchy hippies or, thanks to 'The Craft', vampy goth-style teenagers who wear all black and are obsessed with power and death. Sure, these two groups may very well participate in goddess worship, but that does not mean they all believe this way nor does it require one to be like these two groups to engage in goddess worship. Popular culture, while bringing things more mainstream, doesn't always provide an accurate portrayal. The Goddess isn't just Angelina Jolie or Sharon Stone or Melissa McCarthy, or any other beautiful, intelligent, powerful woman. The Goddess is within and all around, imbuing us with our own spark of divinity to be nurtured and revered as though we were like those aforementioned women.

Incorporating what the Goddess is in everyday life while allowing for what popular culture has made her be as an example of religious integration is an excellent way to preserve the traditional definition of a goddess while allowing for a more personal interpretation to help guide one in their search for their path. Allowing for the belief that the divine Goddess is not only within but also all around, that beauty and intelligence, motherhood and sexuality, strength and vulnerability and kindness are all traits of the Goddess that we as goddess worshippers can possess and exemplify, lends to the idea that reverence is life and can be celebrated many ways.

Ask any Pagan, any Wiccan, any witch, and they will never be able to give you the exact same definition of what goddess worship is to them. There is no cookie-cutter answer that is relevant to every single person who worships the Goddess. Goddess worship is subjective, as is popular culture, and what is relevant to some may not be relevant to others. The allowance for personalization of how someone worships and sees the Goddess is a perk of the neo-pagan movement. It is what someone is comfortable with and what they feel is important to their style of practice.

Popular culture can be seen as a necessary evil in the realm of the Goddess. While the neo-paganism movement is slowly on the rise, information on goddess worship is more prevalent, easily accessible, and more accepted now than ever before. Higher education institutions have more classes that provide a more historical overview of the Goddess and early goddess worship.

Questions can be answered and finding like-minded individuals to practice with or share experiences with is so much easier. Buying tools to help with your practice as well as selling your wares is easier and more accepted. However, with the good comes the bad and there are always the books with misinformation, websites that skew the truth, and individuals who will hurt, rather than help, with their thoughts and beliefs on goddess worship and how you should practice. As with anything in research, religion, and practice; vigilance and striving for the truth rather than blind acceptance is always the wiser and safer path to take.

It is my belief that as a believer and practitioner of goddess worship, allowing the loose definition of goddess to apply to women worthy of the name doesn't hurt, but actually helps raise women to a place of recognition that might not otherwise be given to them. It gives them a sense of power, self-confidence, and awareness of their own self worth they might not have otherwise had. When these women, these Marilyn Monroes, Angelina Jolies, Bettie Pages, Halle Berrys are given the moniker Goddess, they are given a chance to show the divine feminine, to be a physical example of what we, as women, should strive for in not only our secular, but also our non-secular lives. Use these pop culture goddesses to show us that selflessness , kindness, humor, and intelligence is beauty and worthy of worship and reverence. Let popular culture be the conduit that connects the everyday woman to the Goddess and help to give her the desire to learn more about who she is as a goddess. Let popular culture trickle the idea of goddess-like traits to those who might not come to know the Goddess by any other means. Women who practice goddess worship should use the word, the name, Goddess to empower them and give them the strength to allow them to do whatever is their heart's desire. Be a domestic goddess, someone who excels at the keeping of hearth and home, much like Hestia. Be a goddess of love, like Aphrodite. Be a goddess of intellect and wisdom, like Athena or Sophia. Be a goddess of nature, art, and music, much like Cerridwen. It is my belief that women, just as the Goddess, as the other goddesses, are multi-faceted and goddess worship is not only the outer worship of a deity, but also the inner worship of what we see in ourselves as goddess-like. It is up to us as a culture to utilize popular culture as a tool and to help it create a better connection to the Goddess, rather than allowing it to pervert what some call the Divine.

Phoenix Love ~ I am a mother of two mini-goddesses, a daughter, a wife and a sister. Growing up in the South, I came to the Goddess late in life, but that hasn't hindered my love for Her and what She has shown me. I am always learning and I will never claim to know all there is to know about the Goddess and how best to serve her, however I will claim to be a student for life in Her teachings, ever ready to learn her next lesson.

Rewriting the Goddess

Americans don't really have their own Goddesses. There are Native-American Goddesses, but because many modern Pagans are not of native descent, we often go to the Goddess stories of our heritage or, at the very least, what we are drawn to from other cultures. For many Goddess-worshippers, we have become very familiar with these figures and how they play a part in our lives and spirituality. They are recreated in statues sold in shops and on the internet, are illustrated in various depictions for stories and meditation cards, and are rewritten in many anthologies and blogs, their stories modified to fit a contemporary paradigm that wasn't even an option in ancient times when they were first conceived. The theory is that while a wide variety of Goddesses are represented in America as part of Goddess worship, a generic depiction is beginning to emerge where many of the characteristics are blending, motherhood being one of the main attributes, and have replaced the vast differences of each feminine deity.

Goddess traditions in America have adapted, changed, or outright dismissed certain aspects of Goddess figures to suit their own needs. Other theorists see these changes as part of the natural evolution of earth-based religions and spirituality. As modern practitioners, it is essential that we discuss these changes and adaptations so that we can determine the possible effects of those changes.

To find the origins of many Goddesses is very difficult since many of them are an amalgamation of overlapping cultures throughout many centuries and within the context of an oral tradition. Certain elements are added, removed, or expounded upon based on possibly local factors or the individual storyteller's preference. We have no way of knowing. What we can determine, however, is how the documented Goddess and her stories have been adapted to fit within the changing view of women in American culture and what that change has done to Her. This is in no way a negative critique of those changes, but an analysis of that change and a window into the repercussions of changing stories.

One of the first questions is to ask why these changes have even been made. Why is the Goddess rewritten? In an essay entitled 'Contemporary Goddess Thealogy', published in the volume *Shaping New Vision: Gender and Values in American Culture*, Emily Culpepper discussed the feminist view of the Goddess and how that vision has shaped her interpretation. This movement has propelled Goddess work and interpretation, but in the same light the sources pulled for these interpretations have been widespread and varied. Culpepper writes that, 'Feminists interested in Goddesses regard almost any work as a potential source of information and catalyst for insight. None of them is completely adopted; they are freely explored and experimented with.' In the same light, Goddess is difficult to define because part of her strength as a contemporary deity is that she can only be defined by those people who worship her. The Goddess is a combination of her attributes and what those attributes teach us as modern people and that, 'For many a great many women, Goddess means a spectrum of female divinity, extending from the depth of the Self to the sense of a Divine Being who creates the universe.' In another sense, she is often viewed as a channel in which we can reimagine our life and a sense of self.

If Goddess is viewed differently by so many individuals, then it becomes easier to see why and how her stories have been reconfigured and reimagined in so many different ways. Different retellings are not a contemporary construction; because these were oral stories from the beginning; the characteristics most assuredly were changed to meet the needs of the people telling the story and those listening. It has just become a more dramatic shift because we can trace the changes through the written publications.

Meeting the needs of the adherents is the most positive aspect of reimagined tales and Goddess interpretations. Goddess stories teach us. They help us to learn about her culture as well as our culture, and these stories help us to learn about ourselves, like how we could possibly handle complex and difficult situations. Even though the fantastical and magical elements of these stories are not realistic, the lessons sit right beneath the surface, even when the story is so far removed from our own contemporary American culture that a modern Pagan might have difficulty connecting with the lesson.

Adaptions are not new; they are a way to internalize these stories set in time periods that might be so foreign to what we know that it becomes difficult to understand context, and give us another avenue with which to learn. In that adaption, the story structure may change, characters might become less of what they were originally or what we know them to be originally, and even the lesson might change. It might change drastically. What we need to determine what those changes do to the Goddess and be aware of the changes that make in us.

Re-imagining a Goddess

One of my favorite modern interpretations of a Goddess story can be found in the Hindu tradition and has inspired countless people with this new vision. The actual impetus of story was finally documented in a blog post that took the Hindu Goddess Akhilandeshvari, one of the main forms of the Hindu goddess Parvati, and made her into a modern interpretation of a story that so many people can identify. She has become the 'Never-Not-Broken Goddess' from one poignant blog, entitled 'Why lying broken in a pile on your bedroom floor is a good idea' by JC Peters. Documented from a yoga instructor who took the story from oral tellings of his teacher, we have a truly modern interpretation of a little-known Goddess. Many people have baulked at this new interpretation because it is much removed from the original Goddess, what little we know of her, but her inspiration seems to stretch so far that she is recreated as a new almost separate Goddess for people to follow.

Source materials on Akhilandeshvari are very few and might be one of the reasons why her attributes and story are open for such dramatic interpretation. According to those sources she rides on the back of a crocodile and signifies our misdirected fear. Her imperfections are what help to strengthen her, as she is the one who does penitence for her wrongs.

Now, like the Never-Not-Broken Goddess, we have a stronger sense that we as people do not have to be put together all the time; in fact, we cannot grow unless we go through these periods of brokenness that allow us to mourn and then pick up the pieces of our lost souls and put them back together in a new configuration.

New adherents to this Goddess speak of her walking beside them as they continually heal from the fracturedness of the world. They wish to connect with her through tattoo work, something that many Pagans see as a very real and sincere form of devotion. Mental health specialists have taken Akhilandeshvari's new message and connected it to their work with those people who are stuck in depression and need a way to help them re-examine their lives and move out of that fractured existence.

The Softening of Frightening Features

Not all retellings of Goddesses and their stories are so dramatically different, but there are those Goddesses who lend themselves to a reshaping, especially if their homeland is vastly different from what we find in the United States. Yemaya is one such Goddess.

There are several visions of Yemaya throughout the world before she even set foot on the North American continent. She is known in the Yoruba tradition, Cuba, and Brazil in different variants of the Afro-American oral tradition. Her attributes are similar in these countries, but they do pose some differences that lend themselves to various interpretations. Because she is an orisha, she embodies an aspect of nature, in this case the ocean. Like the ocean, Yemaya can be comforting and embracing, but also like the ocean her depths run very deep. Storms can brew suddenly and become violent. This aspect of Goddess is difficult for many modern American audiences to embrace. We prefer our deities loving at all times and not something to fear. Yet, these older versions show a side of life that is just as tangible and important, maybe even more so because they teach us the stark realities of the world.

In most views, Yemaya is the fierce protector of her children, a mother who embodies a strong sense of fortification and instills fear in anyone who threatens those she loves. Anyone who knows this type of mother, is well aware of what that protective spirit can look like, depending on which side of the situation you sit.

When we step outside of these traditions, Yemaya still holds a place among the Goddesses, but she sometimes looks a little different. Her features are soft and the kind and nurturing characteristics are highlighted much more than her fierce protection. She is revered for her loving nature, but not feared for her wrath. As such, several depictions of her are warm and inviting and often stir up different emotions than those considered part of her traditional aspects. Yemaya is a mother goddess, the goddess of home, fertility, love and family. Like water she represents both change and constancy – bringing forth life, protecting it, and changing it as is necessary. Even in a recent Beyonce video we see the softened Yemaya symbolism in the blue and white colors, the flower offering in the water, and the tribute to motherhood alongside the Virgin Mary.

Arianrhod Becomes the Misunderstood Mother

Even in European Goddesses we see an often dramatic change in persona. This is the case in the Welsh Goddess Arianrhod who, in original stories, is a mother who attempts to destroy her son on several instances because she is ashamed of his existence.

This story in the Mabinogi began with Math, who was looking for a new virgin to be his footholder and confidant. Arianrhod revealed that she was a virgin, but did not want to oblige as her uncle's servant. Math tested her word with magic and a child fell from her womb. The child grew instantly and ran to the sea. A second boy was born and Arianrhod's brother Gwydion scooped him up and ran away with him to raise as his own. As the boy grew, Arianrhod refused to give him three necessary things that were traditional gifts from a Celtic mother: a name, arms, and a wife. Therefore, Gwydion and the boy tricked Arianrhod into giving the boy a name (Llew) and duped her into arming him for battle. They were not successful, however, in getting a wife for the boy. Math and Gwydion then cooked up a plan to create a wife out of flowers, and thus begins the story of Blodeweudd. In the end, Llew endured a painful transition in order to seek salvation.

The original story gives us a picture of an unfeeling mother; however, the story can also be interpreted another way, past all the layers of cultural implications and possible misinterpretations.

Modern retellings of the Arianrhod tale have taken a more feminist stance on her story. The three tricks that her uncle and brother performed as punishment for turning away from her son, become three trials that Arianrhod deliberately sets up so that her son, Llew, can become a man. This modern interpretation does not necessarily alter the story, but allows the reader to view the Goddess in a more sympathetic light, one where we begin to see her true motivations. Most characters, be they Gods, Goddesses, heroes, or heroines in Celtic lore have to go through tests or transformations in order to learn or become fully realized. Arianrhod, the Goddess of the divine spark of life, the energy that drives every one of us, was pushing her young son to succeed through many tests. Through cunning and creative thought, he gained those items necessary to become who he was. He also learned that you cannot fashion a woman for yourself, but allow a mate to come to you, if one chooses to do so.

Arianrhod is an aspect of the mother who pushes her children to try for themselves and to even fail, if that is something they need to endure. She was always there to catch Llew; he did not die from the wounds like he thought, but instead shed misconceptions that he held in order to become whole again. These were his trials and a good mother would allow him to get hurt just enough that he would learn from those trials.

Moyra Caldecott's retellings of *Women in Celtic Myth* is one such transformation that highlights a different vision of Arianrhod from a woman duped by her family to give her son what is due to him, to a mother carefully guiding her child to adulthood. Caldecott described this interpretation clearly in the end of the story saying, 'Arianrhod, in her remote castle by the silver sea, was well content that her son has passed through all the tests she had set for him and had become a strong and wise man.'

Implications in Goddess Retellings

Discussions brew around the implications of these retellings, whether moving away from the origins of the tale and the descriptions of the Goddess are detrimental to the tradition or to the Goddess herself or whether they become watered down versions of something richer and more dynamic. In addition, many visual drawings illustrate a more sexualized version of Goddesses, even those whose attributes do not necessarily focus on fertility and love. While these drawings often soften the intimate details of fertilization, some revisions play up the sexual aspect of the seasons to the point of making it an erotic depiction. This creates another layer of implication, especially as America continues our obsession with sex. This is a longer conversation, one that also examines how the retellings have made these Goddesses more relevant to our contemporary lives, and isn't that we imagined the ancient people doing as well; recreating and reimaging, integrating what lessons work within the context of history and culture.

In addition, these changes do not just happen in the US. Retellings, reimaginings, and reinterpretations are not an American construction, but because of our continuing fascination with Goddess lore, we are the most visible in these changes. At a time when Americans are often faulted for damaging cultural stories and conventions, perhaps this might be one area where those changes could be beneficial for those who are using the stories for their own instruction, as long as the origins also remain and are not lost to the centuries of forgotten stories. History, especially ancient history and oral storytelling is not clean and neat. It is very messy and years between translations and visual interpretations can add to the murkiness and nuance of these Goddesses. All deities can change, morph, and transform to accommodate new visions. While there is much to discuss about how those differences might erase what we can only presume as the original intention, we might also look at the new version and see what it can also offer us.

Margo Wolfe is an educator, writer, and member of the Sisterhood of Avalon. She co-ordinates many local events for adults and teenagers, including a Teen CUUPS (Covenant of Unitarian Universalist Pagans) group in PA. Her forthcoming book is entitled, *Turning the Wheel and Mentoring our Pagan Youth: A Curriculum Guide for Instructors of Pagan Teens.*

The Goddess and Reclaiming

In this essay, italicized words are direct quotes from the Principles of Unity.

The values of the Reclaiming tradition stem from our understanding that the earth is alive and all of life is sacred and interconnected. We see the Goddess as immanent in the earth's cycles of birth, growth, death, decay and regeneration. Our practice arises from a deep, spiritual commitment to the earth, to healing and to the linking of magic with political action.

Each of us embodies the divine. Our ultimate spiritual authority is within, and we need no other person to interpret the sacred to us. We foster the questioning attitude, and honor intellectual, spiritual and creative freedom.

We are an evolving, dynamic tradition and proudly call ourselves Witches. Our diverse practices and experiences of the divine weave a tapestry of many different threads. We include those who honor Mysterious Ones, Goddesses, and Gods of myriad expressions, genders, and states of being, remembering that mystery goes beyond form. Our community rituals are participatory and ecstatic, celebrating the cycles of the seasons and our lives, and raising energy for personal, collective and earth healing.
– Taken from Reclaiming's Principles of Unity

These Principles of Unity were first created and consensed upon by the Reclaiming Collective in 1997, and later updated, via consensus, at the BIRCH council meeting at Dandelion 5, an all-Reclaiming gathering, in 2012. This document is seen by many as a guide in the practices of the tradition.

But the story of Reclaiming and its relationship to the Goddess is evolving, and it continues to evolve. It is also the story of the people who practice Reclaiming, who participate in rituals, who are a part of the actions and activism, who teach the core classes, who create community, who stand up for injustice, and who continue to unfold their own mysteries.

In this tradition, we are not bound to working with one deity or one gender or one pantheon, and if we are called to work with one deity or one gender or one pantheon, we are welcome to do so.

The relationship with the Goddess might be one that is personal or public, named or unnamed. It might be a Goddess from a past culture, or we might work with a living tradition, keeping the conversation of cultural appropriation open and these practices with the utmost respect.

Practices

Some of the ways in which we do this work of magic, this work with deity in connection with the wider community, includes ritual, classes, activism, and community.

While this might not the case for everyone who calls themselves a Reclaiming Witch, this is a tradition that seems to comprise people who are active in their magickal practice. They aren't simply doing things for themselves, but have a desire to do something more for the great community.

Whether the work is focused on healing the land or naming imbalances in power, or the work is focused on running around with the little ones or planning a ritual, many Reclaiming folks practice action. Of course, there are times when we move outside of visible places of action and times when we make room for others to step up, but the movement seems to be there – as the Earth needs us to be active.

Ritual

In the practices we have, we include ritual. Ritual can be private or solitary, or it can be public. Though it is encouraged and (often) celebrated to try out new ways of engaging in ritual, the structure most often looks like this:

- Cleansing – cleansing our bodies before the ritual
- Grounding – coming back into ourselves so we might be present and ready
- Casting the Circle – creating the sacred container for the work
- Invoking or calling the Elements – calling on Air, Fire, Water, Earth, and Spirit
- Invoking Spirits of Place, the Land, Time, other entities – calling into the space those beings who might support the work
- Invoking Deity or Deities – invoking Deity in all of their forms
- Tofu – a.k.a. the magickal work of the ritual – trance, ritual drama, meditation, something else...
- Raising energy with a spiral dance – often, there is a song that is sung to raise energy while dancing a spiral dance, as well as drumming
- Benediction – a blessing of the work
- Food blessing and sharing – a blessing of food to nourish us in the work going out into the world
- Devocations – thanking the beings who have been invoked and called in, releasing and opening the circle

Anyone who considers themselves to be a Reclaiming Witch can be a priestess in a ritual, and hold a ritual role. This is, again, a part of the non-hierarchical structure of the tradition, and the desire to share power in all areas of community. While it is certainly encouraged that the priestess has an understanding of the ritual and its intention, everyone is welcome to be a part of many ritual planning processes.

Rituals are spaces in which spellwork happens, and they are ecstatic workings in which everyone is encouraged to participate at their own level of comfort. There are clear intentions for the workings, and those who are not willing to uphold or support the intention are able to leave the circle without any questions asked or any judgment.

Because rituals are places where mysterious things can happen, there are also moments in which an invocation may not be as expected. Some invocations might include singing, while others might include dance or drama. Other callings might encourage those attending the ritual to help, while others may not.

In doing so, we invite in the possibility of divine play, as well as the child self, the part of us that is not always welcome to 'such serious things.' We welcome the possibility of one person's reverence looking different from another's reverence. And we might learn something new about our own practice.

There are moments in ritual where there may also be opportunities to commune with the divine while in ecstatic states of consciousness or while a priestess is in a light possession state, called 'in aspect.'

In addition, some practices of devotion in ritual might include seeing others in the ritual with the eyes of the deity. One might dance for devotion, or drum, or sing, or chant, or make noises, or make altars, etc.

Ritual is a space of mystery and it is also a space in which many things happen to aid in healing, in changing the world, in bringing together community, or in breaking old stories.

Magick is the place where ritual lands, and the place where Reclaiming Witches will get the opportunity to move into ecstatic states, to the places where we might fear to go, and to the places this world needs us to go.

Classes

We know that everyone can do the life-changing, world-renewing work of magic, the art of changing consciousness at will. We strive to teach and practice in ways that foster personal and collective empowerment, to model shared power and to open leadership roles to all. We make decisions by consensus, and balance individual autonomy with social responsibility.

In addition to ritual, working with the Goddess and other deities and other beings includes classes. In the tradition of Reclaiming, there are several standard classes that began in 1980 with Starhawk and Diane Baker. They started to teach Elements of Magic, realizing there were many who were interested in creating their own rituals.

From there, the students wanted to learn more, so more classes formed, and from those classes, students became teachers and then initiates, and the tradition was born. (Note: the story of how Reclaiming began is one that is nebulous, not because it's unknown, but there are different memories that have been passed on. The best way to find out more is to ask around to see what stories there are, as we are lucky to have many of the founders still active today, without attachment to the 'one true story.')

The classes are taught with at least two teachers, allowing for the modeling of shared power and to further help dismantle the power structure around us. Classes are taught often in private residences, while others may be taught online or in public settings.

In addition, there are also Witch Camps that are located around the world, and some are for those aged 18 and older, while others are for families and others are still emerging. These are often longer intensives in which a person might be immersed in ritual and magick for a week at a time, creating a new community in the space of nature and then bringing the wisdom of this experience out into the world.

At the time of writing, the classes that have built the

foundation of Reclaiming's practices include: Elements of Magic; Iron Pentacle; Pentacle of Pearl; and Rites of Passage.

Elements of Magic is where the basics of ritual are taught and explored. Iron Pentacle follows the Feri practice of this pentacle, and the points of Sex, Pride, Self, Power, and Passion, and the work of shadow, of internal introspection. Pentacle of Pearl includes the points: Love, Law, Wisdom, Liberty, and Knowledge, and the work of brightness and moving out into community. Rites of Passage includes dreamwork and looking at our stories to see how we might rewrite them and re-rite them as we move through transitions.

Of course, these are just my experiences, and these classes can hold and have held other experiences as well. The different teachers will bring different slants to the work, so know these are basic descriptions.

A person might choose to take these classes in order, from Elements to Rites, or they might choose to only take one or two. Or they might take them over and over, as each new experience may present a new layer of understanding.

It is not necessary for a person to take these classes, though some groups within Reclaiming encourage them to build a foundation for teaching and leadership roles.

Classes are a place where many have also started covens and study groups, and where lifelong friendships have begun.

Activism

Our tradition honors the wild, and calls for service to the earth and the community. We value peace and practice non-violence, in keeping with the Rede, 'Harm none, and do what you will.' We work for all forms of justice: environmental, social, political, racial, gender and economic. Our feminism includes a radical analysis of power, seeing all systems of oppression as interrelated, rooted in structures of domination and control.

The active energy of Reclaiming is clearly seen in the activism that is part of many community member's public practices, as well as their private lives. Not only might groups of Reclaiming Witches be seen at protests in San Francisco, the WTO, or other locations, but also there are many others who speak up for the oppressed and engage in changing community one conversation at a time.

This is a tradition that wants to find out how to support those who may be held down by the overculture, and how to actively challenge the current societal norms. Often, this looks like organizing actions and non-violent protests in public settings. It might also look like sharing information and bringing up these conversations at rituals, at classes, or in everyday conversation.

Community

We welcome all genders, all gender histories, all races, all ages and sexual orientations and all those differences of life situation, background, and ability that increase our diversity. We strive to make our public rituals and events accessible and safe. We try to balance the need to be justly compensated for our labor with our commitment to make our work available to people of all economic levels.

All living beings are worthy of respect. All are supported by the sacred elements of air, fire, water and earth. We work to create and sustain communities and cultures that embody our values, that can help to heal the wounds of the earth and her peoples, and that can sustain us and nurture future generations.

There is a place in Reclaiming for many voices and many bodies and expressions of self. One of the things that brought me to this tradition was its devotion to community building and diversity. While there are so many places in our lives where we are judged for who we are and what we look like, Reclaiming is a place to be accepted.

To be sure, people are people. And while you might not get along with everyone all the time, this is a tradition that values the diversity of our experiences. As stated in the Principles of Unity, Reclaiming accepts and supports all genders, all gender histories, all races, all ages, and all sexual orientations. We welcome all life situations and all economic levels, and we have conversations about how we can support each other – and create sustainable communities.

We reach out to people in the local communities through conversation, through websites, and through social media. Often, we might find new community members through larger public events, like the annual Spiral Dance ritual. But we also reach out by helping communities that are in need of help, and by contributing to conversations at Pantheacon or via Facebook.

Community is something that is built, and Reclaiming actively works to build and to understand how to make connections stronger. This is not a perfect tradition, of course, and we continue to strive to do more to reach out and to help those who might need support and visibility and acceptance.

The Future

The thought of the future of Reclaiming is exciting and, yet, the world seems to be in need of many more things than any one tradition of Witchcraft might ever be able to achieve. Though there is no set plan for Reclaiming and what it might do going forward in years to come, here is what seems to be true:

- Reclaiming will continue to offer rituals and classes. There are many communities around the world that already offer classes and public rituals, helping to connect people to the core classes and to connect people to groups of people who share the same values.
- Reclaiming will spread into new communities and areas.

With communities now growing in Australia, it's clear that Reclaiming can continue to emerge in new locations and is likely poised to find new groups who are ready to do more.

- Reclaiming will begin to offer new workshops/discussions/events. Since this is an ever-evolving tradition, it's safe to say that new classes and other offerings will begin to be offered in response to community needs.

- Reclaiming will continue to stand up for the oppressed and to speak up against misuse of power. The fight to help others who feel marginalized, the fight to question power structures, and the fight to save the Earth are all fights that will continue to be at the forefront of many Reclaiming Witches' minds (as well as many in community).

The future of Reclaiming looks like one of action, intention, magic, and community. Together we are the ones we have been waiting for, to quote Alice Walker.

Irisanya is a Reclaiming Witch, initiate, priestess, teacher, and drummer, as well as an often-vegan, shapeshifter, shadow stalker, invocateur, beginning ukulele player, and Sagittarius devoted to Aphrodite, Iris, and Hecate. She has been published in *Paganism 101*, *Naming the Goddess*, and *Pagan Planet*, and makes her living in California as a writer. Her website is at www.irisanya.com.

A Dream of the Wise Woman's Comeback: Priestessing for Goddess in Today's America

I glimpsed her in a dream one night, bits of mugwort, hops, and seashells tangled in her hair, dressed in an old maroon and grey raglan baseball jersey, deep, dark blue jeans with studs like the stars of a summer sky and her cuffs rolled up. Her dirt-stained, bare, calloused feet poking out from underneath them. She had ancient eyes set into a complex tapestry of crow's feet that danced, changing the tempo of their choreography as her expression shifted from joy to sorrow, ecstasy to rage. Even as those eyes held the wisdom of ages, her smile was like a toddler's, so hopeful and open. But her hands – her hands told me everything she was capable of then and now.

She was a wise woman, one of many, shifting her form with the liquid passage of time. And she came to teach me about all that is required when one is called to her path in this country, at this time. Service to Calling, to Community, to Goddess. A commitment to work in the world as healer, protector, advocate, ritualist of the everyday, and conduit for community connection. Hers is not the way of high magic. She is no High Priestess with a lineage of formal instruction and initiation. Hers is the way of stick and stone, blossom and bone. Hers is the way of radical grace in service to whomever Goddess puts in her path; of grounded optimism in a time and a nation that desperately craves creative solutions. She is the grass and the roots. And she is rising.

The American wise women are coming into their own again, reclaiming their trade. Are you destined to be one of them? Are you already walking her path, dusting off her tracks and making them your own?

Together, you and I, let's explore this exciting, pivotal time in the American wise woman's resurgence. Lessons await in the landscape of each of the wise woman's major roles, juxtaposed against our modern mess of an America. We need more of her, this woman who is healer, protector, advocate, everyday ritualist, and conduit of community. We crave a taste of her work.

But we must also take time to pause and reflect, to remain open to whether or not one or more of these wise woman callings are manifesting in our own lives and how each of us might engage that calling further, making ourselves an integral part of her comeback. Perhaps ours as well. To begin with, consider the following:

- *When you read the words 'wise woman' what springs to mind? Don't think, just flow. Say them out loud to yourself – what images, concepts, roles, feelings, and other sensory feedback emerge?*
- *What are your understandings of the historic wise woman? What sources are these understandings predicated upon? What is helpful to learn and remember about yesterday's wise woman in light of today's America?*
- *What does a modern American wise woman look like to you? What functions would she serve in your community? Do you see yourself in her at all?*

Wise Woman as Healer

In that vivid dream of mine, when she opened her hands, she shook spikey mugwort blossoms from her hair into her palms. Twisting one stalk between her elderberry-stained fingertips, she grinned and offered me one of the oldest healing plants known to wise women. She gestured, inviting me to add it to her cauldron, which looked an awful lot like my own enamel cast iron Dutch oven. And she taught me that the most important part of crafting healing potions is listening deeply to those who seek them.

Wise women healers come in all shapes and sizes these days. If you sit and think about it for a moment, you probably know plenty. These are women Goddess has charged with serving as doctors, nurses, midwives, herbalists, first responders, counselors, chiropractors, acupuncturists, body and energy workers and more. They are all crossing paths with the wise woman's work. But there are also those who we find ourselves seeking when we need healing who have no such credentials, who stand in liminal places radiating soft, but powerfully unmistakable presence. We come to them when we are hurting, tired, wounded, distressed.

In our relationship with Her, Goddess often asks us to examine our lives. She encourages us to identify those wounds that drain us. She empowers us to seek healing. In doing so, we come to know what it takes to heal. There are those of us who grow through our own healing. Goddess often charges us with assisting in the healing of those who come after us. Some of us will train, formally educating ourselves in one or more healing modalities. Some of us will find ourselves taking a more autodidactic route as individuals from our community seek us out for that thing we do – the thing they hardly have a name for any more, but know in their bones they still need.

With Goddess' help, we release the fear of being healed and our apprehension about working as healers in a deeply wounded country. We learn as we go how to use the talents She's blessed us with to offer succor, counsel, and safe passage through wounding or dis-ease. Our client base expands to include those outside our specific traditions, and even outside our Goddess-centered faith. We allow ourselves to be Her healing hands and by doing so, heal ourselves, our clients, our communities, and our country in rippling waves of divine works. The more wise women who take up the healing charge, the more ripples.

Spend some time considering:

- *How many healers do you know, which ones do you seek out, and what makes them so good at what they do?*

- *What healing skills do you feel today's American wise woman needs to have at her disposal? What was the last wound or disease you healed for yourself or another? What skills did you rely on to do so?*
- *How are you called to heal and be healed in the communities of our wounded nation?*

Where can you get started? How does one just jump into this process of becoming a healer in service? Try this suggestion, perhaps. Have you ever made fire cider? It's a powerful American folk remedy – a tonic that should be in the hip pocket of every wise woman worth her horseradish. There are plenty of recipes to choose from out there in the mystical ether of the internet, but the basics remain the same – chopped and grated garlic, onion, horseradish, ginger, lemon, chili pepper, turmeric, and rosemary soaked in a quart glass jar of apple cider vinegar for a good lunar month. Then, strain out the solids, mix in raw honey to taste and use to help cure what ails you.

The best wise women healers also know laughter is a powerful remedy. As are music, friendship, and time spent with circles of women. To add that extra wise woman's kick to your own healing brew, invite others to gather with you. Build an interfaith community altar dedicated to fire and healing. Share an intention to craft this folk remedy with each other. Make extra batches to give away to those in need of them. See each other through the Tradition-transcending rite of passage that is grating those fresh horseradish roots together. Become a gathering of turmeric-stained healers. And listen for the wise women. For in those moments, they are with you and in you.

Wise Woman as Protector

As our dream potion of mugwort, compassion, and healing continued to brew, her head came up, sensing a disturbance in her world I could not see or hear. Her hand, her gifted, healing hand, closed over the hilt of the dagger at her side that was shoved through the wide belt loop at her hip. The same dagger with which she gathered healing herbs and branches. For the first time, I saw it clearly. A pommel of jet, the crescent moon of the silver knuckle bow, a sturdy leather-wrapped grip, and the keen steel edge of her guardianship. If her land was being threatened, she stood ready; capable of defending of her territory.

Those of us who know Goddess, know how often we find Her in the earth. The swaying song of the trees, the dance of fireflies over a pond, mist rising from the surface to kiss the cattails. Wildflowers rioting across open meadow. Lenticular clouds crowning glorious mountain tops. We can see, hear, smell, touch and taste Her in those moments. We also know those moments are dying. Industry, greed, and thoughtlessness ravage Her sacred spaces, jeopardizing our health and welfare as they do so. Wise women are one rank of her protectors.

As part of the defense of wildflowers, mountain tops, and those who need them, we also have another noble notion to defend. That of grounded optimism. That of hope. Even as she bared her teeth and reached for that dagger at her side, the wise woman pressed her free hand to my heart and reminded me that all is never lost. That we are clever, cunning women who are capable of creating new and powerful Goddess-centered solutions that defend without destruction. Underneath this lifetime's everyday wear, wise women's fierce bones are green. How green are your bones today? Do you:

- *Reduce, reuse, recycle and rethink how you approach consumption in your life as a protector of the green?*
- *Spend time in the green spaces in your community, getting to know them, watching over them, encouraging others to do the same?*
- *Envision yourself as a protector? If so, what is it you protect? How can you craft creative solutions to the threats you feel called*

to defend against?

Not sure where to start? Worried about how expensive it seems like it can be to 'go green'? Fair enough. But make a list of as many ideas as possible for small, everyday, inexpensive ways you can green up your life just a touch more. Ask Goddess to inspire you. The goal here is to become a better, wiser protector of this nation's sacred lands even when you're not flush and able to do the weekly shop at the organic grocer or incredibly fit and mobile.

Start small. Do what you can. That is all the wise women ask of you.

Wise Woman as Advocate

Shoved through the opposite belt loop of her jeans, I next noticed a tool I had not anticipated. As silver as the guard of her dagger, but as modern as that dagger was ancient, there hung a glossy microphone. *What's a wise woman to do with a microphone?* I thought. Her six-word answer rang in my head in reply: *Speak truth to power, of course.*

A wise woman, she told me, is cunning, yes, but always strives to live in right action through her service to others. She has an obligation to Goddess to oppose injustice, to speak for those who cannot, to be an ally to the oppressed, to relentlessly seek reforms where they are needed. She does not always change the world all at once. Wise women know the power of radical grace; of doing the small thing that eases small pains and brings small justices to bear.

The wise woman collects household goods donations for refugee resettlement or domestic violence recovery programs. She takes a regular shift at her local food bank or soup kitchen. She volunteers at voter registration drives. She helps those who want to find ways to be of service to locate opportunities in their own communities that need their talents. She educates others, bringing to light injustice and oppression in her own backyard. She doesn't take 'no,' or, 'it's always been this way, it's hopeless,' or, 'we can't fix this,' for an answer. She is an active advocate for social justice and caring for the members of humanity that inhabit her community.

Ask yourself:

- *Where do you see suffering and oppression in your own community?*
- *What small acts of radical grace could you undertake to ease or eliminate that today?*
- *Why must an American wise woman embrace the active advocacy her historic European predecessor may have shied away from in the past?*

See yourself as capable of co-ordinating a canned food drive. Or of dropping off extra blankets at a local homeless shelter. Make even the smallest effort to speak truth to power part of your daily practice and you make yourself a tool of Goddess. The beginning activist's guide, *Grassroots* by Jennifer Baumgardner and Amy Richards, is a great place to start in learning the wise woman's art of advocacy and activism. So is just getting out there and doing it.

Wise Woman as Ritualist

She took her dagger and her microphone out of their loops, laid them down beside the bubbling Dutch oven, and beckoned at me. I followed her into the mists. When I caught up with her, she had bound up her hair with Spanish moss and draped a simple black linen cloak about her shoulders. She was lighting candles. Women stepped out of the mists around me, creating a circle that enveloped us into its perimeter. She smiled. And ushered us all into sacred space.

More and more, American women crave ritual not tied to

specific spiritual traditions in their lives. Mother-baby blessings are increasingly replacing baby showers as the pre-birth ritual of choice. Death doulas and soul midwives are stepping into ritual roles of service created by the burgeoning home death movement. The labyrinth has made a huge comeback.

All acts of love are Her rituals.

To facilitate a mother-baby blessing, to lead a candlelit community labyrinth walk, to create entirely new ways to mark the dying of friends or family – these are acts of Goddess-centered love. These are not high magicks, with pageantry, doctrinally-requisite tools, specific intricate invocations. This is the territory of the everyday ritualist. We are all capable of doing this work as long as we move from the Goddess-blessed love we know resides within us.

Imagine what it would look like if you:

- *Facilitated a mother-baby blessing for the next willing friend or family member expecting a wee one?*
- *Issued an open invitation for your community to attend a simple, moonlit labyrinth walk?*
- *Created a brand new, low magic ritual to mark an occasion for a loved one?*
- *Saw yourself as Goddess' priestess in your community at-large?*

Think about what little, everyday rituals are important to you. Think about how you might offer those beautiful ritual moments in a way that might make them important to others in your community, too.

Wise Woman as Conduit of Community

Before the dream of the wise woman visited me, there was a little community gathering event I started to hold around every equinox and solstice no matter where I lived at the time. Those who've attended over the years know it as Witch's Night In –

WNI, for short. I invite every woman I am connected to in my community, mixing social circles with fearless abandon. We bring together an amazing array of food, drink, ages, backgrounds, spiritual traditions, and experiences. We build a seasonal community altar representative of all of our combined faith traditions. I read cards for anyone who brings me something sparkly. We laugh, cry, listen and are heard well into the night.

As my early WNI gatherings became a regular occurrence in my community, I began to see how, in some small way, this little gathering was a return to the days when one would periodically seek out the wise woman for healing or counsel. Except, in this case, the most phenomenal thing was occurring. Witch's Night In was empowering all the women in attendance to be wise women in their own traditions, serving each other and their community. Allowing us all the opportunity to see divinity in each other.

This sharing of such fertile wisdom in sacred, interfaith space across traditions cultivates understanding, compassion, and peace in our small corner of the world. In that space, we begin to engage deeper, tougher topics together. We create a space where a woman from one faith tradition might be able to ask a woman from a very different faith tradition any questions she might have about her practice. I continue to read cards for anyone who asks me on those evenings and we build some truly beautiful community altars as the seasons turn.

Within the container that Witch's Night In provides, Pagan and Muslim, Christian and Hindu, Druze and Wiccan can come together, learn from each other, listen and be heard as they speak with the voices of wise women in their cultures and their faiths. Our activities are more varied now too. Sometimes, I still read cards. A favorite activity in the past has been reading our tea leaves together. Another time, we drew labyrinths and mandalas. Occasionally, we simply eat, drink, and share our lives; our stories.

These American wise women in the making have taught and

continue to teach me about the beauty and strength inherent in their unique, diverse spiritual lives. For every woman who has ever been to a Witch's Night In and every woman who might one day join me in that magical space, wherever in the world I can continue to create it, I am grateful.

And so I invite you, wise woman-in-the-making:

- *Take this simple little WNI-style community gathering and make it your own. Make it come alive in whatever corner of this country you live in today. Contribute to peaceweaving the fabric of community back together in a divided nation and ask Goddess for Her blessing on your work.*

Wise Woman Returns

Early the next morning, as I floated on the edge of consciousness, she came to me one last time. She reached for me and when I looked down, my hands and her hands were suddenly so similar. She smiled that half-smile, equal parts knowing and innocence. With a quick kiss on the cheek, she shooed me out of the dream and on my way. We know what to do. The wise women have already carved out the way. We have only to bring it out of history and dream time in order to make it what we need it to be today.

With every batch of fire cider brewed, every birth and death attended, every labyrinth walk facilitated, every mother-baby blessing woven together, every Witch's Night In hosted, we grow stronger and more visible in communities and our ever-expanding circles of wise women. With every organic garden grown, every new recycling program started, every tree planted in the local parks, every protest organized, every voter registration drive completed, every meal served in soup kitchens, every injustice called out, every reform finally secured, we speak more clearly and work more closely with Goddess in America.

So, ask yourself one last time:

- *What does a modern American wise woman look like to you? What functions would she serve in your community? Do you see yourself in her after all?*

Kate Brunner is a writer, healer, ritualist, wise woman-in-the-making, and member of The Sisterhood of Avalon. Kate is also a presenter at Red Tents and women's spirituality retreats. She hosts seasonal women's gatherings, facilitates labyrinth rituals, and leads workshops on an assortment of women's spirituality topics.

The Goth Goddess

In every tradition and pantheon, the dark goddess exists...

The Morrighan from the Celtic – a triple goddess of war, battle, and strife. She appears as a washer woman, washing the clothes of those warriors who would die in battle. Often manifesting as a black bird (crow or raven), she feasts on the dead who litter the fields of war. She is winged, armor-clad, and fierce.

Kali in the Hindu tradition – the one who possesses both the power of creation and destruction, often seen as 'mother', but a mother who is as inescapable as time, and also inspires knowledge of her power. She has long, flowing black hair that is free from convention of any sort. She dances on the white chest of Shiva, the pure primal existence. She has four arms and wears a garland of skulls.

Lilith from the Christian doctrine (via Sumerian origins) – a woman who owned her own sexuality and refused to be dominated by her male mate, who was later demonized and accused of eating babies. Often pictured as a slick, blood covered demon, she is the antithesis of what a good, compassionate woman 'should' be. She is personified as sexual, terrifying, and violent.

Bast in the Egyptian pantheon – a shape shifter who can see in dark places, with a sexual appetite to rival any, but also a protector. The cat-headed goddess is sleek, black, and armed with fangs and claws.

The examples could go on and on, but they have several common characteristics:

1. Sexuality. The darker goddesses are beautiful in whatever form they take, some quite terrifying, and have a sexual appetite that is independent of puritanical values or societal constraints. These women enjoy and explore their

sexuality with no real barriers. They feel and express their beauty as part of their sexuality, rather than as divorced from it.

2. Power. Without doubt, the most prevalent characteristic of this group of divinity is their clear and prevalent power. They are warriors, protectors, destroyers, and creators. They are often clad in armor, protected by fierce creatures, or winged.

3. Related to intuition. Most of these goddesses are closely related to dreams, intuition, clairvoyance, divination, and 'seeing' in the darkness. They expand and broaden physical sight to include the internal and ethereal and spiritual realms. They may commune with the dead, carry messages and information, and predict the future.

What woman would NOT want to connect to this group of powerful, beautiful, sexual, intelligent, creative, and intuitive goddesses?

The modern Goth in American culture embraces all of the characteristics of the dark goddesses, while also engaging and embracing the darkness, itself. In that darkness, there is room for fantasy and mythos not contained in any particular pantheon or religious tradition. For instance, the vampire, the werewolf, the shape shifters, and creatures of all sorts who exist in the night.

The same modern Goth Goddess enfolds herself in the transition and mystery of death in a way that celebrates life at its fullest. They host Victorian teas in cemeteries. They actively participate in a wide variety of cosplay events. They may embrace body modifications – piercing, tattooing, corset training, and more. To understand the evolution of this movement, it is well worth evaluating its relatively short past...

The early Goth movement grew out of the punk rock culture of the 1960s and 1970s in America. By the end of the 1970s, the Goth movement was born. In its earliest incarnation, it was often called 'positive punk' and was far livelier than its current phase. Bands such as *Sisters of Mercy, Fields of Nephilim, Southern Death Cult, and Sex Gang Children* ushered the movement into the awareness of the larger public. Richard North's article (New Musical Express, Feb., 1983) carried in the idea of the 'positive punk' movement. Lisa from the band *Blood and Roses* is reported as having discussed the idea of 'all the forces are still there underneath, bubbling, steaming, fermenting. The instinct, ritual, and ceremony are rising again in everyday life.' (The History of Goth, online)

Can we pinpoint a place where the Goth movement sprung to life, barreling from the dirt and dark into the larger society? No. It was more of a quiet evolution, a seedling growing more than an eruption. In many ways, it is the commingling of a certain style of music (romantic, dark, emotive), fashion (ranging from pin-up to Victorian), and those people (mystical, cosplayers, fantasists) who were drawn to explore alternative approaches to life through the process of playing with the idea of death which truly transformed into a culture.

Perhaps it was those who felt disenfranchised by the punk movement of the day – the romantics who found the clothing too frilly, the punkers who felt the music too light. Whatever their origins, the movement has endured. In conversation with modern day Goth adherents, some consistent patterns appear.

HM

HM, a 30-something female, talked about feeling out of place as a child in her private school. Her parents owned a small business in which she was required to work on hours that she wasn't attending school with far wealthier and more privileged children. She described the Goth community as 'on the fringe' and made up largely of 'artistic types' who 'welcomed anyone and everyone.' Here, she found 'friends of many different backgrounds' and was largely attracted to the 'look' that was embraced. HM also noted that the culture seemed to be a haven for those with mental differences, with many diagnosed with one type of mental illness or another. HM reported that she struggles with depression and felt as though the 'music and other kids understood how I felt.' As an adult woman in today's society, HM described how she continues to maintain her Goth fashion as an understated 'retired Goth' version of her formerly more open self… 'I've learned how to keep the basics of Goth…You can spot them from across the room. We all still carry it with us to some degree…I do still rock my pigtails.' (Personal interview, 2015)

Lady Strange

In her goth application on a Live Journal blog called Gothloyalty (online, 11-11-2008 post), Lady Strange (TW, age 47) listed among her responses the answer to this question, 'Why do you want to be here and what in your opinion makes you 'Gothic Royalty?'' by replying, 'As to why, it would be nice to converse with people who actually know Peter Murphy did something OTHER than 'Cuts You Up' and understand that all the eyeliner in the world won't make you Goth if you don't 'get it.' As to the Royalty part, really Darling, isn't it obvious?' This pervasive attitude of being above the understanding of the uninitiated is common to nearly all subcultures from sociological and anthropological stand-points, and is critical to the makeup of any culture – the idea of shared norms, values, and beliefs.

In response to an inquiry about what drew her to the Goth aesthetic, Lady Strange responded, 'I don't recall a time when I wasn't drawn to both the finer things in life AND the darker side of them. I've always been at home in museums, Victorian era homes, and cemeteries. I've always preferred modes of dress that hearkened back to a more elegant time.' This also reminds us that there are MANY Goth aesthetics, including 'Victorian Vampire', which is the preference of our Lady Strange; but, there is also an evolution of Goth into some new offspring, including: cyber,

Lolita, rivet head, graver, emo, and more. Perhaps, most notable are the modern-day emo participants whose clothing runs back to the earliest part of the positive punk movement with band tees, skinny jeans, lots of black, and hair covering most of the face, but not very long in the back. But, that is fodder for another essay!

It is perhaps Lady Strange's response to the question, 'What is Goth?' that is most telling and explanatory: 'A respect for the Beauty in the Shadow, the understanding that 'alone' is not necessarily lonely; the grace and elegance of a bygone era. In more modern context, it means a connection – a relationship with [like-minded] people who are tolerant of views and choices 'outside the box.' The ability to insult someone and have them thank you for it because you were so very eloquent... In the end, I'm 'Goth' for much the same reasons I'm pagan. I tried to not be, and it never felt right. It never felt like 'me.'" This, is how I choose to think of Goth – something beautiful and ferocious, self-possessed and prescient. (Personal Interview, 2015; blog entry, 2008)

Another common bond among the Goth community is a clear attachment to all things supernatural, particularly those of darker imagery...the Fae of Irish tradition who were frightful and feuding, not the fluffy Disney© version; shape shifters; venomous creatures of all sorts; vampires (there is, in fact, an entire subculture within the Goth community of those who live as vamps); even the fluffys could be considered a cosplay off-shoot in some circles. As well, there are some norms that can be traced throughout the movement: clove cigarettes, incense, gravestone rubbings and a general like of all things cemetery, dark poetry full of angst and strife, black (LOTS of black – lipstick, hair, eyeliner, clothing, boots, leather, velvet, and lace), corsets (male and female, of course), and more.

Most enduring, of course, is the music: Sisters of Mercy, Concrete Blonde, Switchblade Symphony, The CruxShadows, Unto Ashes, Ego Likeness, and more. And, certainly, a cult-like following of some movies: The Crow and Bram Stoker's Dracula among them.

The fascination with death and darkness is far less sinister than one would imagine. Instead, it is more consistent with the passage through the underworld experienced by many of the dark goddesses. It is the delight in the cycle of life, including its demise, and an understanding of the value of the time of rest in between. It is the transformation that precedes rebirth. Examples are abundant. In the Sumerian poem (circa 1900BCE) The Descent of Inanna, this is chronicled quite clearly:

From the great above, she opened her ear to the great below…

My lady abandoned heaven and earth to descend to the underworld…

In Uruk, she abandoned her temple…

She gathered together the seven me…with the me in her possession, she prepared herself…

She placed the shugurra , the crown of the steppe, on her head. She arranged the dark locks of hair across her forehead. She tied the small lapis beads around her neck, Let the double strand of beads fall to her breast, and wrapped the royal robe around her body. She daubed her eyes with ointment called 'Let him come, Let him come.' Bound the breastplate called 'Come man, come!' around her chest, Slipped the gold ring over her wrist, And took the lapis measuring rod and line in her hand…

Wisely, Inanna directs her faithful servant to where help may be found should she not return. And, she continues on her journey.

Met at the gate by Neti, the gatekeeper, Inanna must answer this question, 'If you are truly Inanna, Queen of Heaven,/On your way to the East,/Why has your heart led you on the road from which no traveler returns?'

Inanna replies that she's come to her sister, Ereshkigal, the

Queen of the Underworld, for the funeral rites of her husband, the Bull of Heaven. And, upon Ereshkigal's orders, Neti required Inanna to bare herself, relinquishing each of the seven me (gifts of the gods) on the descent. Inanna consented.

Inanna entered the underworld naked and bowed.

The annuna, the judges of the underworld, surrounded her. They passed judgment against her. Then Ereshkigal fastened on Inanna the eye of death. She spoke against her the word of wrath. She uttered against her the cry of guilt. She struck her. Inanna was turned into a corpse – a piece of rotting meat and was hung from a hook on the wall.

(Wolkstein and Kramer, *Inanna Queen of Heaven and Earth*, 1983)

Whether we consider the journey to be symbolic or mythological, it is, undoubtedly, a journey to one's self – one's authentic self – which is accepted without adornment, without pretense, and with that which is true and real and genuine. This is the central aspect of the modern Goth Goddess – a woman who leaves behind all those things that they have laid upon themselves, the masks of falsity to hide behind, the societal roles and expectations forced upon us by norms not our own.

The Goth Goddess is a woman under her own power, celebrating her sexuality, her warrior aspect, as well as that of the sage, the philosopher, the adventurer, and the intellect.

She has shaken loose those extraneous items to reveal her essence, hard won by self-awareness and self-study, to be unbound in the world as she sees it...as she sees fit. She is without boundary.

She is beautiful, whatever her shape.
She is powerful, whatever her strength.
She is fearsome, whatever her dynamism.

She is unafraid.
She is FREE.

Michele Leigh Warch is a witch, scholar, priestess, author, blogger, metaphysical and energy practitioner, teacher, wife, mother, grandmother, herbalist, oneirocritic, and founder of Temple of Energetics (a private community for metaphysical practitioners) who lives on the Mid-Atlantic coast of America.

Goddess in her Own Right. The Role of Women in America Today

There are many women who have helped shape America into what She is today. These courageous women fought against all odds for the freedom and equality of the oppressed. They are the heroines of this land I call home; and are the very Spirit of Liberty, the Essence of Freedom, and the Soul of Bravery. They are our ancestors – our blood – our Sisters.

Though there are many women I would like to honor, due to space I have chosen nine Ladies to grace this essay. Why nine? In ancient lore there are a number of Sisterhoods of nine Goddesses or Faery Women.

- The Nine Muses of Greek mythology: Clio, Euterpe, Thalia, Melpomeni, Terpsicore, Erato, Polymnia, Ourania and Calliope.
- The Nine Sisters of Avalon: Moronoe, Mazoe, Gliten, Gliton, Glitonea, Tyronoe, Thiton, Thiten and Morgan le Fay.
- The Nine Ladies of the Lake (from *Ladies of the Lake* by *Caitlin and John Matthews*): Igraine, Guinevere, Morgan, Argante, Nimue, Enid, Kundry and Ragnell.
- The Nine Maidens whose breath kindles the fire beneath the Cauldron of Annwn.
- The Nine Witches of Gloucester and the Nine Priestesses of the Island of Sein.

In keeping with the Sacredness of Nine, I have chosen these Nine Ladies of America to honor. These women are Goddesses in their own right, they are our American Queens of Sovereignty. Their names are known throughout American history and are still honored and remembered today for the great deeds they accomplished. These women are beautiful and brave, strong and adventurous, honorable and just. They are: The Nine Ladies of America...

Queen of Beauty

Josephine Baker (June 3, 1906-April 12,1975) *'Surely the day will come when color means nothing more than the skin tone, when religion is seen uniquely as a way to speak one's soul, when birth places have the weight of a throw of dice and all men are born free, when understanding breeds love and brotherhood.'*

She was known as Black Pearl, the Bronze Venus and the Creole Goddess. Sultry and exotic, her song and dance captured the hearts of many. American by birth, French by heart and soul, Josephine Baker was the epitome of beauty, earning her more than a thousand marriage proposals. It was her passionate and sultry dance that won her fame. She stunned the audience with her feather skirt in the dance performance of *Danse Sauvage* with dance partner Joe Alex and stole the stage while dancing in a skirt made of 16 bananas in her performance of *La Folie du Jour*.

Josephine Baker was not just known for her exotic beauty, she was a fierce opponent in the fight against racism. Though she renounced her American citizenship due to the blatant racism in her birth country and finding herself falsely accused of being a communist, she would return to help support the Civil Rights Movement alongside Martin Luther King Jr. She was a lifelong advocate of the equality of all. Adopting 12 children from different countries, she called them her Rainbow Tribe. Her hopes were to prove that people of different races could live together in peace and harmony.

Josephine Baker showed us that there is beauty to be found everywhere; she lived her dream of dance and song. She was a beautiful mother to many, setting the example that love knows no color. She was stunning, graceful in her beauty, both inside and out. Josephine Baker, the Bronze Venus, will always be remembered for her sultry beauty and her fierce love for equal rights.

Ways to Honor the Queen of Beauty

- May 20th is known as Josephine Baker Day in honor of her participation in the March on Washington in 1963.
- Support the Red Cross. Josephine Baker worked for the Red Cross during World War II during the occupation of France.
- Stand up for equal rights and the injustice of racism.
- Live your dreams!
- See the beauty within.
- Read: *Josephine: The Dazzling Life of Josephine Baker* by Patricia Hruby Powell and Christian Robinson; and *Josephine Baker in Art and Life: The Icon and the Image* by Bennetta Jules-Rosette.

Lady Justice

Rosa Parks (February 4, 1913-October 24, 2005) 'Stand for something or you will fall for anything. Today's mighty oak is yesterday's nut that held its ground.'

Growing up in segregated America can takes its toll on the mightiest of people. Rosa Parks, a black woman from Montgomery, AL, stood her ground one December day. After a long, tiring day at work on December 1, 1955, Rosa Parks, sitting quietly during her bus ride home, was told to give up her seat to a white passenger. When she refused, explaining that she shouldn't have to stand up during the ride, the bus driver called the police, having her arrested on the spot. What ensued was the start of a revolution for justice and equality.

Known as the Montgomery Bus Boycott, this protest led to months of near empty buses, crippling the transit's finances. The black community fought for their rights, demanding equality and the end of segregation laws. In June 1956, the district court of Montgomery declared racial segregation laws unconstitutional. The U.S. Supreme Court upheld the ruling on November 13, 1956.

Rosa Parks, forever strong and ready to fight for justice, found many hardships in Montgomery after the fight for the end of segregation. Both she and her husband lost their jobs, leading the two of them and Rosa Park's mother to start a new life in Detroit, Michigan. There she served on the board of the Planned Parenthood Federation of America.

Rosa Parks will be forever remembered for her strong character, she is an icon for all women of American. She reminds us to stand up for what we believe in, for what is true and just.

Ways to Honor Lady Justice

- Support the *Rosa and Raymond Parks Institute for Self-Development* and the *Pathways to Freedom* bus tour.
- Fight for justice, freedom and equal rights for minorities.
- Stand up for your rights.
- Her birthday, February 4th, is often held in remembrance of her.
- Visit her statue at the U.S. Capitol Building.
- Read her memoirs: *Rosa Parks: My Story* and *Quiet Strength*.

Queen of Adventure

Amelia Earhart (July24, 1897- c. January 5, 1939) 'Courage is the price that life exacts for granting peace.' — 'Adventure is worthwhile in itself.'

When I think of an adventurous life, I am immediately brought to mind of the fabulously daring Amelia Earhart. Known as 'Lady Lindy', in 1923 she was the 16th woman to be issued a pilot's license. In 1928, Amelia Earhart became the first woman to fly across the Atlantic Ocean and the first person to fly over both the

Atlantic and Pacific oceans.

Amelia Earhart defied the perception of women in the early 1900s, proving that we can Dream the Impossible. She showed us that we, as women, with courage and self-reliance, can break the bonds of patriarchal views that keep us from living our dreams.

In 1937, Amelia Earhart and her navigator, Fred Noonan, mysteriously disappeared while trying to circumnavigate the globe around the equator. Though she was officially pronounced dead in January of 1939, Amelia Earhart still lives on in the hopes and dreams of many women. She was a woman who knew what she wanted in life and fought for the rights and independence of the American Woman.

Ways to honor the Queen of Adventure
- July 24th (her birthday), Amelia Earhart Day
- Live your dreams passionately and fully!
- Always embrace an adventurous life!
- Be independent and true to yourself.
- Have courage and stand up for Women's Rights.
- Read: *Amelia Lost: The Life and Disappearance of Amelia Earhart* by Candice Fleming and *The Sound of Wings: The Life of Amelia Earhart* by Mary S. Lovell.

Lady Freedom
Harriet Tubman (c. 1820-March 10, 1913) 'I freed thousands of slaves, and could have freed thousands more, if they had known they were slaves.' — 'Every great dream begins with a dreamer. Always remember, you have within you the strength, the patience, and the passion to reach for the stars to change the world.'

She was known as the female Moses, leading many slaves to freedom by way of the Underground Railroad. As a one of the leaders in the abolitionist movement, Harriet Tubman became the most famous 'conductor' on this secret network of safe houses for slaves seeking freedom. She escaped from slavery after many years of physical abuse, some of which would cause permanent damage. She escaped with two of her brothers who soon decided to return for fear of their safety. After seeing to their safe return, Harriet set off on her own for a lifelong dream of freedom.

After a long journey, using the Underground Railroad, she finally reached Philadelphia. She then made it her mission to rescue as many from her family as she could. Though she was a wanted woman, she continued her work on the Underground Railroad, freeing thousands of slaves.

Harriet Tubman was a woman who loved her people fiercely; she wanted to see them all freed and spent her life working toward that goal. She became an American icon and still inspires many in the Civil Rights Movement today.

Ways to honor Lady Freedom

- Visit the Harriet Tubman home in Auburn and the Harriet Tubman Museum in Cambridge.
- Fight for the rights of the oppressed.
- Live your life in freedom and honor.
- Honor her on March 10th, the date of her death.
- Read: *Scenes in the Life of Harriet Tubman* by Sarah H. Bradford and *Harriet Tubman: The Road to Freedom* by Catherine Clinton.

Our Lady of the Sacred Feminine

Susan B. Anthony (February 15, 1820-March 13, 1906) 'It was we, the people; not we, the white male citizens; nor yet we, the male citizens; but we, the whole people who formed the Union.' — 'The fact is, woman are in chains, and their servitude is all the more debasing because they do not realize it.'

Along with her friend Elizabeth Cody Stanton, Susan B. Anthony formed the New York State Woman's Rights Committee and eventually founded the National Woman Suffrage Association. As a lifelong activist, she was deeply committed to not only the Woman's Rights Movement, but the Abolitionist, Labor, and Temperance movements as well.

In 1872, after advocating for the women's right to vote, Susan B. Anthony illegally voted; leading to her arrest and a fine of $100. In protest, she refused to pay that fine. Sadly, in 1906 Susan B. Anthony died before she could see her efforts achieved. In 1920 the 19th Amendment was passed, giving women the right to vote. Susan B. Anthony spent her adult life fighting for the rights of women for equality in the voting booths, marriage and the work force. She stood up for what she knew was true and just and never gave up the fight.

Ways to honor Our Lady of the Sacred Feminine

- VOTE! In every election! She and her supporters fought fiercely for the rights of the American woman.
- Stand up and fight for women's rights today. This battle still rages on.
- Visit the National Susan B. Anthony Museum and House in Rochester, NY.
- Honor her on her birthday, February 15th.
- Read: *Failure Is Impossible: Susan B. Anthony in Her Own Words* by Lynn Sherr and Elizabeth Cady Stanton, and *Susan B. Anthony: A Friendship That Changed the World* by Penny Coleman.

The Warrior Queen

Buffalo Calf Road Woman (c.1850-1878)
'A nation is not conquered
Until the hearts of its women
Are on the ground.
Then it is done, no matter
How brave its warriors

Or how strong its weapons.'
Traditional Cheyenne saying from *Buffalo Calf Road Women: The Story of a Warrior of the Little Bighorn* by Rosemary Agonito and Joseph Agonito.

When her brother, Chief Comes in Sight, fell from his horse after it was shot in the Battle of Rosebud (1876), Buffalo Calf Road Woman broke from the ranks on her war horse, rescuing her brother and rallying her Cheyenne tribe to victory. This battle is known as The Fight When the Girl Saved Her Brother.

Buffalo Calf Road Woman would continue to fight for the freedom and safety of her tribe, fighting alongside her husband, Black Coyote. She is credited with knocking Custer from his horse in the Battle of the Little Big Horn (Custer's Last Stand). Forever a warrior, Buffalo Calf Road Woman never shied from battle. She fought for the land that was rightfully theirs; a land that was being constantly raped and pillaged by the white men who refused to acknowledge its Sacredness.

Ways to honor The Warrior Queen

- Fight for what is right and true.
- Remember that this land we live on is Sacred.
- Support the Native Americans and don't appropriate their religion and ancient ways.
- Read: *Buffalo Calf Road Woman: The Story Of A Warrior Of The Little Bighorn* by Rosemary Agonito and Joseph Agonito.

Our Lady of Song

Ella Fitzgerald (April 25, 1918-June 15, 1996) 'Just don't give up trying to do what you really want to do. Where there is love and inspiration, I don't think you can go wrong.'— 'The only thing better than singing is more singing.'

Known as the *First Lady of Song* and *Lady Ella*, Ella Fitzgerald became the first black woman to win a Grammy Award, winning a total of 13 Grammys in her long career as a jazz singer and vocalist. She lived and breathed the world of song, capturing the hearts of America with her sultry voice. Being called the 'High Priestess of Song' by Mel Tome, Ella Fitzgerald became the Queen of 'scatting'.

Shy and self-conscience of her appearance, Ella Fitzgerald felt her anxieties melt away as she took the stage. At times she had to face racial discrimination, but she had many allies. Not only did her manager, Norman Ganz, stand up for civil rights and demanded equal treatment for all his musicians, Marilyn Monroe once helped her pack a popular night club by promising to sit front stage every night that Ella performed.

She was the *Queen of Jazz* and the *First Lady of Song*; Lady Ella continues to fill our hearts with song through the more than 200 albums she recorded. She lived her dream passionately with a deep love for life.

Ways to honor Our Lady of Song

- Sing your song loudly and proudly (even if you can't hold a tune).
- Live your dreams.
- Support the Ella Fitzgerald Charitable Foundation; created by the First Lady of Song herself to help people of all races, cultures and beliefs.
- Help the children of the world. Ella was an advocate for Child Welfare.
- Read: *Ella Fitzgerald: First Lady of Song* by Katherine E. Krohn.
- And, of course, listen to her many soul filled songs.

Earth Warrior
Rachel Carson (May 27, 1907-April 14, 1964) 'We stand now where

two roads diverge. But unlike the roads in Robert Frost's poem, they are not equally fair. The road we have travelled is deceptively easy, a smooth superhighway on which we progress with great speed, but at its end lies disaster. The other fork in the road/the one less traveled by/offers our last, our only chance to reach a destination that assures the preservation of the earth.'— 'Those who dwell among the beauties and mysteries of the earth are never alone or weary of life.'

Rachel Carson, one of nation's first Environmental Activists, stood strong in her convictions within a male-dominated scientific community. As a concerned biologist, she warned the world of the dangerous effects of fertilizers and pesticides. She would later die of cancer caused by the environmental hazards of which she fought so hard to bring about awareness. Her arguments against the pesticides, namely DDT, led to much ridicule from her fellow scientists.

It was through her book, *Silent Spring*, that Rachel Carson raised awareness in the Environmental Movement. To this day her influential book has led many to the path of Green Living. She was a true Earth Warrior, taking the lead in the battle against the chemicals that harm the Earth, our Sacred Home.

Ways to Honor the Earth Warrior

- Honor the Sacredness of our Land by fighting against the use of harmful pesticides and other chemicals that continue to poison Earth.
- Reduce, reuse, and recycle.
- Strive for a Greener Life.
- Read *Silent Spring* by Rachel Carson.

The First Lady

Eleanor Roosevelt (October 11, 1884-November 7, 1962) 'A woman is like a tea bag – you never know how strong she is until she gets in hot water.'— 'Beautiful young people are acts of nature, but beautiful old people are works of art.' — 'Life was meant to be lived, and curiosity must be kept alive. One must never, for whatever reason, turn his back on life.'

The longest serving First Lady of the United States, Eleanor Roosevelt would be named the First Lady of the World by Harry S. Truman. She was not just the wife of the long serving President Franklin D. Roosevelt, Eleanor Roosevelt was a writer and a Human Rights and Woman's Rights Activist. She was outspoken in American politics and had her own newspaper column, 'My Day'. Eleanor, also known as Ellie and Little Nell, stood against racial discrimination and rallied for the rights of many.

After her husband's death, Eleanor Roosevelt continued to serve America. She was a delegate to the United Nations General Assembly, and became a chair in the United Nation's Human Rights Commission. Always outspoken, Eleanor Roosevelt continues to inspire the woman of America. Through her, we have learned to fight for human, civil, and woman's rights with dignity and conviction. She was a true leader in the Human Rights movement and will be forever held in high esteem as the First Lady of America.

Ways to honor The First Lady

- Speak your truth.
- Fight for the Rights of All.
- Live your life with dignity and grace.
- Be active in your life; live it well.
- Read: *You Learn By Living* by Eleanor Roosevelt, *The Autobiography of Eleanor Roosevelt* by Eleanor Roosevelt, and *Memorable Quotations: Eleanor Roosevelt* by Diana J. Dell.

These women are our ancestors – our blood – our Sisters. They are the true Queens of America, leading the way to Freedom and

Justice. These Nine Ladies of America are not the only women we can honor as our Queens, there are more from our heritage and many more to come. The women who are fighting for our Rights and Freedoms today will be the Queens of America tomorrow. Rejoice in our Sacredness, for we are all Queens and Goddesses in our own right.

Vivienne Moss is a solitary witch who resides in a small Indiana town. She spends her days brewing up trouble with her two daughters, and her nights casting spells. When she's not writing, you'll find her taking long walks through the forest or strolling through the local cemetery. A lover of all things occult, Vivienne dedicates her time to the study of esoteric knowledge. Vivienne's hope is to share the magic of the World with fellow seekers of Witchdom. Vivienne is the author of *Pagan Portals – Hekate*.

Have you read *Naming the Goddess*?

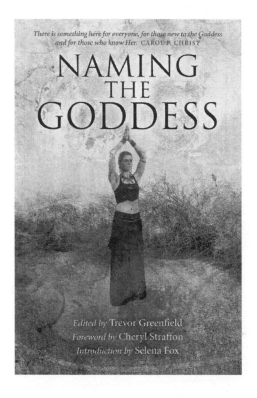

Naming the Goddess is written by more than eighty adherents and scholars of Goddess and Goddess Spirituality, and includes contributions from Selena Fox, Kathy Jones, Caroline Wise and Rachel Patterson. Part 1 is a series of critical essays focusing upon contemporary Goddess issues. Part 2 is a spiritual gazetteer featuring more than seventy Goddesses.

There is something here for everyone, for those new to the Goddess and for those who know Her. Carol P. Christ, author of *Rebirth of the Goddess*.

978-1-78279-476-9 (paperback)
978-1-78279-475-2 (e-book)

Other Moon Books You May Enjoy

The Morrigan, Morgan Daimler
On shadowed wings and in raven's call, meet the ancient Irish
goddess of war, battle, prophecy, death, sovereignty, and magic.
978-1-78279-833-0 (paperback)
978-1-78279-834-7 (e-book)

The Cailleach, Rachel Patterson
Goddess of the ancestors, wisdom that comes with age, the
weather, time, shape shifting and winter.
978-1-78535-322-2 (paperback
978-1-78535-323-9 (e-book)

Hekate, Vivienne Moss
The Goddess of Witches, Queen of Shades and Shadows, and
the ever-eternal Dark Muse haunts the pages of this poetic
devotional, enchanting those who love Her with the charm only
this Dark Goddess can bring.
978-1-78535-161-7 (paperback)
978-1-78535-162-4 (e-book)

Brigid, Morgan Daimler
An introduction to the Goddess Brigid focusing on her history
and myth as well as her modern devotion and worship.
978-1-78535-320-8 (paperback)
978-1-78535-321-5 (e-book)

Elen of the Ways, Elen Sentier
The reindeer goddess of the ancient Boreal forest is shrouded in
mystery...follow her deer-trods to rediscover her old ways.
978-1-78099-559-5 (paperback)
978-1-78099-560-1 (e-book)

Moon Books invites you to begin or deepen your encounter with
Paganism, in all its rich, creative, flourishing forms.